HONORING THE SEASONS

Quilts from Japan's Quilt House Yama

Takako Onoyama

Translated by Robert L. Neal

MISSION STATEMENT

WE ARE DEDICATED TO PROVIDING QUALITY PRODUCTS AND SERVICES THAT INSPIRE CREATIVITY. WE WORK TOGETHER TO ENRICH THE LIVES WE TOUCH.

That Patchwork Place is a financially responsible ESOP company.

Honoring the Seasons:
Quilts from Japan's Quilt House Yama

That Patchwork Place, Inc., PO Box 118,
Bothell, WA 98041-0118 USA

Printed in Hong Kong

01 00 99 98 97 96 6 5 4 3 2 1

Library of Congress Cataloging-in-Publication Data
Onoyama. Takako,
Honoring the seasons : quilts from Japan's Quilt House Yama / Takako Onoyama.
p. cm.
ISBN 1-56477-169-5
1. Patchwork—Patterns. 2. Quilting—Patterns. 3. Patchwork—Japan. 4. Quilting—Japan. I. Title.
TT835.066 1996
746.46'041—dc20 96-31345
CIP

ACKNOWLEDGMENTS

Special thanks to the Edo-Tokyo Open Air Art Museum for use of their grounds for the photography in this book. Located in Koganei-shi Tokyo, this wonderful museum keeps the spirit of traditional Japanese lifestyles alive. Many of the architectural exhibits were moved brick by brick and preserved with great care and accuracy.

Credits

Editor-in-Chief
Kerry I. Hoffman

Technical Editor
Laura M. Reinstatler

Managing Editor
Judy Petry

Design Director
Cheryl Stevenson

Copy Editor
Liz McGehee

Proofreader
Melissa Riesland

Illustrators
Brian Metz, Laurel Strand, Robin Strobel

Photographer
Brent Kane

Cover Designer
Kay Green

Text Designer
Sandy Wing

Production Assistant
Claudia L'Heureux

Additional Photography
Akinori Miyashita, Nobuhiko Honma Cheryl Brown

Translation
Robert L. Neal

TABLE OF CONTENTS

Introduction

The history of Quilt House Yama is also the history of Takako Onoyama. On March 10, 1976, Quilt House Yama began with just two employees and me, the owner. It rained all day as people with umbrellas passed by. From the corners of their eyes, they peeked with interest at the new store. At that time, only friends of mine and my employees would gather—they were more like members of a gossip group than customers.

The handmade crafts and patchwork merchandise reflected only my taste, with no obvious concept. I had to explain the term "patchwork" to each customer. The pioneer-era quilts in America were far more creative than the patchwork on display in our store. In spite of this, I started offering classes.

The fabric available in Japan at the time was manufactured for apparel, so it wasn't really appropriate for hand quilting. The search for my taste in fabric proved difficult and showed me I would have to create my own designs. So, I filled my washing machine with hot water and started dyeing fabric. Although this old-fashioned washing machine did its best and put out more power than it was designed for, it finally choked on the lint and stopped working. The resulting hand-dyed fabric, however, proved very popular and sold well. (I continued to buy washing machines until I found someone that could dye the fabric for me.)

To piece patchwork projects by hand took so much time that the products cost too much. In 1978, I traveled to the United States to learn how to make quilts quickly by using a sewing machine. Although it had been twenty years since I studied English, I decided to attend the West Coast Quilt Conference. A Japanese proverb states, "Reading something a hundred times is not as good as seeing it once." In this case, the wealth of knowledge I attained was comparable to learning how to harvest grapes in a desert and make wine!

▲ *Office staff*

◀ *Sales staff*

This shows just a few of the many treasures at Quilt House Yama. ▶

After that, our store changed at a rapid pace. The supply of American fabric and quilting supplies started to increase. At the time, Japan was promoting exports. The weak Japanese yen, strict customs officials, and high import costs made it difficult to import goods. Despite these challenges, customers were attracted to finding rare merchandise, and the popularity of patchwork quilting grew. Recently, it has become easier to import American fabric, and there are many new shops. Today, most of my time is dedicated to maintaining a large variety of the latest American prints.

In 1979, I made another trip to the United States to attend my first International Quilt Market and Festival. It was held at the Shamrock Hilton in Houston, Texas. I was the only attendee from Japan and actively communicated with the American quilters. I learned many things at this show and made many contacts.

This overseas trip was a turning point in my life. Back in Japan, being knowledgeable of rare overseas information, I enjoyed increasing opportunities to publish what I knew. It was great advertising for my shop.

A cozy corner offers a quiet spot to browse through some of the latest books. ▼

Being the first person to open a quilt shop in Japan, I was a true pioneer. I willingly put all my efforts into my business. I brought many instructors from the United States to teach classes, including Roberta Horton, Judith Montano, Ellie Sienkiewicz, and Jinny Beyer. Students enjoyed attending these free-spirited, rewarding classes and were excited to be a part of this new creative energy.

I also arranged many quilt exhibitions in Japan and overseas. A highlight for me was curating the Denver Art Museum collection, which was a great success. This exhibition set a new record for attendance at the department store in which it was held.

After that, Quilt House Yama (affectionately known as Yama-san) continued to expand its business. I opened new shops in Sapporo and Fujisawa, and developed three affiliated branches. With these new stores, I greatly increased imports.

The year 1990 saw many changes. I became a member of a project to start patchwork correspondence courses. This involved developing new products, marketing materials, and checking the students' finished products. This project was an incredible success, enrolling more than 100,000 students in five years.

The work at the Tokyo store increased, making it difficult to stay involved with both the classes and management, so I felt it necessary to sell the branch outlets. I then started wholesaling. In this way, the main store became the center of business operations, with the mail-order business developing into a more independent entity.

In 1976, while the United States celebrated the two-hundredth anniversary of its independence, the first quilt shop in Japan opened. In March of 1996, Quilt House Yama celebrated its twentieth anniversary, along with the twenty-year history of American quilting in Japan. During these years, women's independence took a step forward: quilt shops opened throughout Japan, almost all of which are run by women.

◀ *From the top:* Seminole Patchwork, Family Patchwork, Simple Patchwork, Patchwork Gifts, *and* Patchwork without Templates

Patchwork and Quilting in Japan

Throughout history, people have gathered objects from their past and present-day culture. In Aomori, the northernmost region of mainland Japan, archaeologists have discovered needles fashioned from deer and boar bones. These needles, along with cases to keep them in, date back some fifty-five hundred years. Some objects—including ancient artifacts, famous structures, and fine works of art—have become world treasures and are preserved with great care.

Folk art is another aspect of culture often preserved. Coming from nameless members of the populace and reflecting their lifestyles, this art is much like plants that have pushed their way up through cracks in the pavement, flourishing along the sides of roads and blooming with tiny flowers. Folk art naturally coexists with and embellishes everyday life.

Quilting is a form of folk art. Many of the earliest quilts were made in the United States for utilitarian and economic reasons, but their beauty and creativity have captivated many people. Although the designs and intended purposes may differ from country to country, treasured antique quilts have been well cared for and mended or overhauled when necessary.

▼ *Mt. Fuji*

Sashiko joins layers of fabrics with strong quilting stitches.

Japanese fiber arts also have practical origins. The strenuous work of fishermen placed stringent demands on their apparel. These demands led to a simple but sturdy garment, although the design may have differed from region to region. To make full use of the sparse fabric supply, the innovative people of the time made work clothes from leftover fabric strips. Durable fabrics from aprons, sacks, arm covers, sandals, and rags were often used in the construction of a *sashiko* half coat. *Sashiko*, a traditional Japanese technique similar to quilting, has been around since the Nara period (710–794 A.D.). It involves overlapping layers of fabric to insulate and strengthen them, then joining the layers with a strong quilting stitch.

Most of these projects were utilitarian and somewhat lacking in creativity. However, a form of piecework survived the tides of time in an unusual place. Garment makers for the temples continued a style of piecework when making the priests' robes. From as early as the Nara period, the traditional outer garment for priests has been a *kimono* made by piecing together strips of cloth.

A *kimono* undergarment, worn by a general named Kenshin Uesugi about 1560 A.D., was made by piecing lavish strips of cloth. And in Kanazawa of Ishikawa prefecture, there is a type of children's *kimono* that is made by sewing together many swatches of cloth (called *Kaga no Hyakutoku)*. Once the children grew into healthy adulthood, those who had prayed for their health would offer the *kimono* to the temple in appreciation. To this day, these *kimono* are preserved with great care in the temples.

In modern-day Japan, piecework is not uncommon. Japanese *kimono* have a simple, straight-cut design, so the leftover swatches are easy to piece. These leftovers are often sewn together to make covers for futon mattresses and cushions, decorative toy balls, *kimono*, and undergarments, among other things. When I was a girl, making such items was considered part of homemaking.

Besides piecework, *oshie*—a form of appliqué resembling decoupage—is used for decoration. Developed at the end of the Edo period (1603–1867 A.D.) and the beginning of the Meiji period (1868–1912 A.D.), it uses silk crepe (called *chirimen*) and was the only form of women's sewing done solely for hobby. As with English paper piecing, this method requires making templates from a traditional Japanese paper (called *washi*). *Chirimen* is wrapped around each template, then positioned and glued to a surface to make a three-dimensional design. *Oshie* expresses a delicate beauty and has graced framed pictures, folding screens, and decorative paddles, among other items.

When I was a child, I used to play the traditional New Year's game of *hanetsuki*, a girls' game very similar to badminton. *Hanetsuki* requires a beautifully decorated battledore (paddle) called a *hagoita*. The finishing touches of *oshie* on this paddle look like floral appliqué. When I played *hanetsuki*, I would wear a beautiful *kimono* and become very involved in the game, so I'm sure you can imagine what the *kimono* would look like after the game!

▲ *Hagoita, a paddle used in a badminton-like game, shows an appliqué technique called oshie.*

◀ Kaga no Hyakutoku *jacket.*

Kichijoji

My home and shop are located in Kichijoji, which lies in the western part of Tokyo. Kichijoji is accessible by four train lines and several bus lines. A bustling town, it overflows with vitality. Several colleges and high schools are found nearby. Kichijoji Temple stood in a town in Tokyo known as Kamagome. Unfortunately, in 1657 the temple burned down in the great fire that devastated Tokyo, then known as Edo. Many people living near Kichijoji Temple sought shelter in this area, then took up residence, forming the town of Kichijoji.

Historically, this area was a leisure spot for the shogun. During the Edo period, the elite shogunate would participate in falconry here. After Edo became known as Tokyo, this quiet rural area with its lush greenery became popular with painters, writers, and other artists. Many famous people came to live here, and many works of art blossomed.

▲ *Inokashira Park in Kichijoji*

In the 1960s, the roads near Kichijoji were developed and the town changed rapidly. Department stores, boutiques, restaurants, and coffee shops popped up, seemingly overnight, and the main street was, and still is, always overflowing with people.

One of the reasons this town is loved by so many is that Inokashira Park lies within three minutes' walk of the train station. This beautiful park has a wonderful zoo and an extensive pond brimming with *koi*, or carp. It has become routine for my husband and me to walk our dog each morning in Inokashira Park. On sunny days, you can always hear children's laughter. If you decide to take a walk through the trees, you'll come across an open-air art museum with many sculptures and a tearoom. Depending on the time of year, different kinds of flowers bloom there, giving me a feel for the changing seasons.

The most festive time of the year is spring, when the cherry blossoms are in their glory. Many people gather both day and night to admire the flowers and to party beneath the cherry trees, eating, drinking, and participating in the festivities.

The younger crowd has shortened the name Kichijoji to Joji, and I think their influence will keep Joji an innovative town. My favorite pastime is eating, so I'm looking forward to the many new restaurants the future holds in store.

Quilt House Yama
1976~1996
20th Anniversary
Kogire Utanokai

▲ *Members of Kogire Uta no Kai*

◀ *Twentieth Anniversary Quilt*

Takako Onoyama

Patch Poem Society

This beautiful quilt (at left and above) is very precious to me. It was made by the twenty-four members of our quilt group to commemorate the twentieth anniversary of Quilt House Yama. The name of our group is *kogire uta no kai*, which translated means "Patch Poem Society." We held our first meeting fourteen years ago.

Members of the group share ideas about quiltmaking, hold exhibits, and plan international exchange gatherings. The monthly meeting is always exciting.

Each Rose of Sharon block has the signature of one of our members. The circle pattern represents our endless friendship, and the red ribbon stands for the long, hard road that led to opening the first quilt shop in Japan. I will treasure this quilt for the rest of my life.

Metric Conversion

1 inch (") = 2.54 centimeters

1 yard = 0.9144 meter

To convert from inches to centimeters, multiply the number of inches by 2.54.

To convert from yards to meters, multiply the number of yards by .9144.

▲ Hinamatsuri
(Girl's Day)
by Takako Onoyama

◀ Bingatazome
(Japanese Stenciling Print) by Youko Morita

Harukaze ni Notte ▶
(Ride the Spring Breeze)
by Fujie Fukuhara

Octagon Block

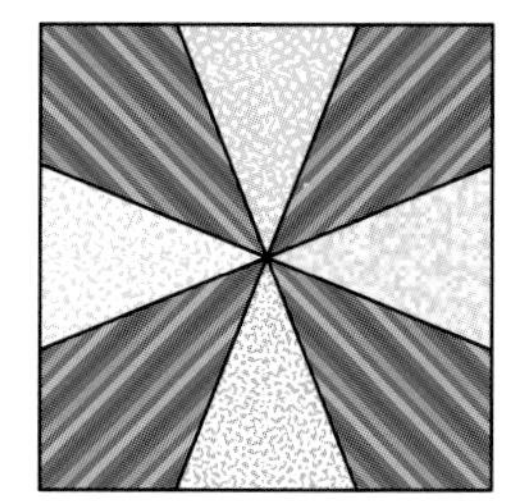

Alternate Block

Bingatazome (Japanese Stenciling Print)

Finished quilt size: 72½" x 42½"
Finished block size: 7½" x 7½"

Bingata, *a traditional form of dyeing that requires stencils, glue, and dye, was developed in Okinawa, an island in southern Japan. The colors are plentiful and bright, typical of designs created under the brilliant southern sun. Today, the prints are used in many kinds of folk art other than* kimono. *Looking at Okinawa geographically, its proximity to China explains the many Chinese influences seen in the prints.*

Materials: 44"-wide fabric

11 squares, each 7½" x 7½", large-scale floral prints for *Bingata* blocks (octagon A)
1½ yds. navy blue–and-white stripe for block corners (kite D and triangle E)
¼ yd. *each* of 11 assorted small-scale prints with light background or use scraps (triangle C)
¼ yd. purple solid for *Bingata* blocks (strip B)
⅛ yd. yellow solid (trapezoid F)
⅛ yd. orange solid (trapezoid G)
½ yd. green solid (pieces H and I)
1¼ yds. rust print for outer border
13 yds. of striped 2"-wide fabric OR 2⅜ yds. gray stripe for inner border (cut along the lengthwise grain)
Assorted motifs from floral and butterfly prints for appliqué
4¼ yds. for backing
47" x 78" piece of batting

Cutting

Cut all strips across the width of the fabric from selvage to selvage unless otherwise noted. There are no templates for A and B. Use the templates on page 19 for pieces C–H, and on page 18 for piece I.

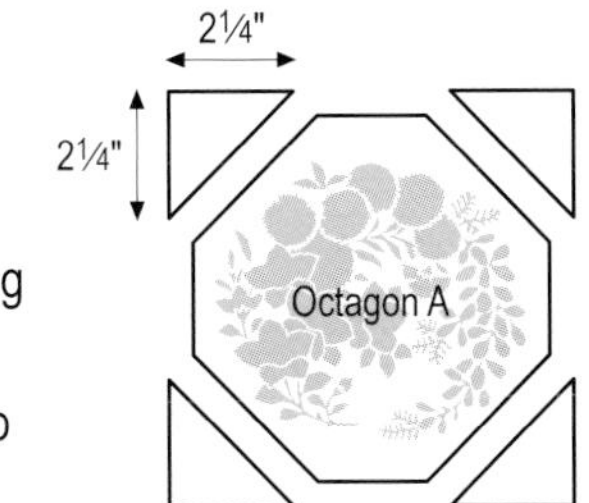

On each of the 7½" floral squares, mark the edges 2¼" from each corner. Draw a cutting line, connecting the 2 points on each corner. Trim the corners to make octagon A.

From the navy blue–and-white striped fabric, cut:
64 kite D
64 triangle E

Note: Follow the layout diagram for templates so the stripes for each D/E unit align when they are sewn together.

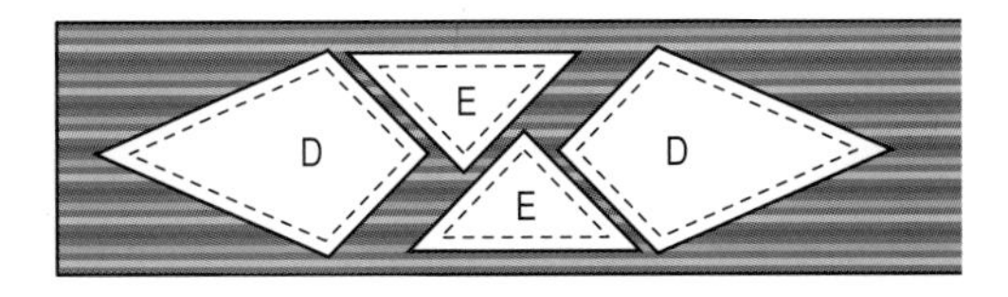

From the assorted small-scale prints, cut:
52 triangle C

From the purple solid, cut:
10 strips, each ¾" wide. From the strips, cut a total of 88 segments, each 4½" long.

From the yellow solid, cut:
2 strips, each 1½" wide. From these strips, cut 8 trapezoid F.

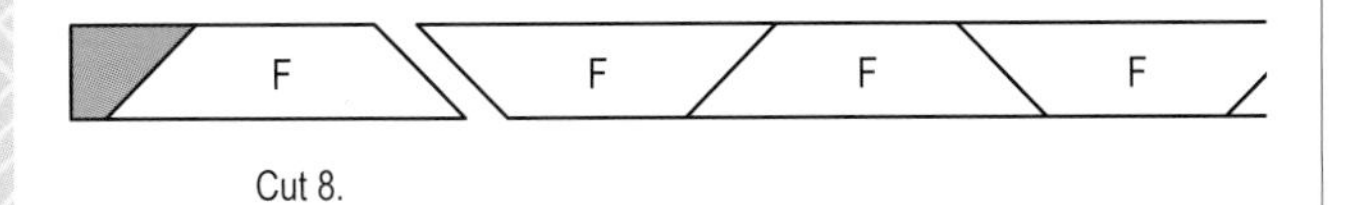

Cut 8.

From the orange solid, cut:
2 strips, each 1¾" wide. From these strips, cut 8 trapezoid G. From the remaining fabric, cut 4 triangle E for corners.

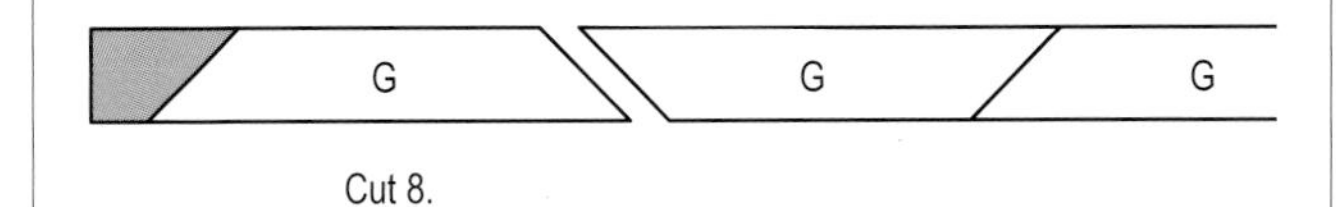

Cut 8.

From the green solid, cut:
8 strips, each 2" x 18". Fold each strip in half crosswise, align Template H on the fold, and cut.

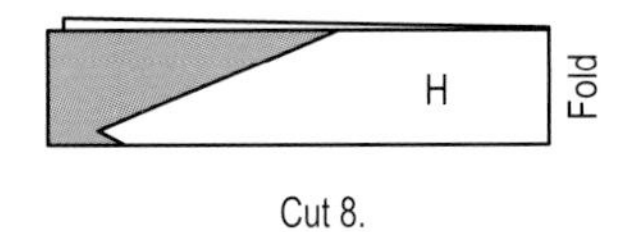

Cut 8.

2 strips, each 2" wide. From these strips, cut piece I and piece I reversed for corners.

Cut 4 I and 4 I reversed.

From the gray stripe, cut from the lengthwise grain:
2 strips, each 1¾" x 67", for side inner border
2 strips, each 1¾"x 37", for top and bottom inner border
2 strips, each 2" x 77", for side binding
2 strips, each 2" x 47", for top and bottom binding

From the rust print, cut:
8 strips, each 5" wide, for outer border

Assembly

Note: Handle with care when sewing and pressing to avoid distorting the bias edges of the pieces and blocks.

1. To make each octagon block, sew a ¾" x 4½" strip B to each side of octagon A in a clockwise direction. After adding each strip, press the seam allowances toward the outer edges. Trim the strip ends as shown.

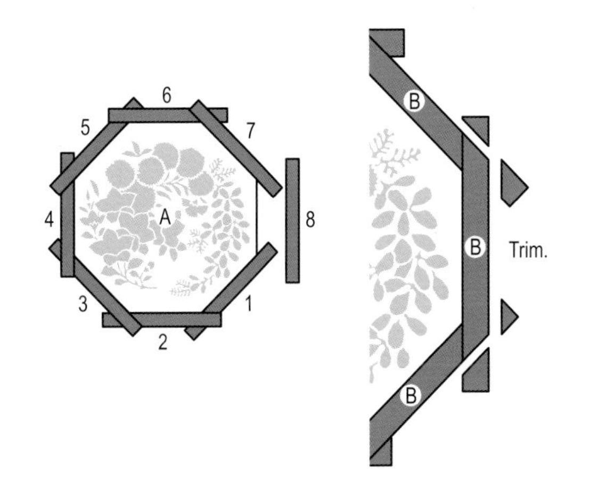

2. Sew a navy blue–and-white triangle E to each corner of the section made in step 1 to complete the octagon block. Press seam allowances toward triangle E.

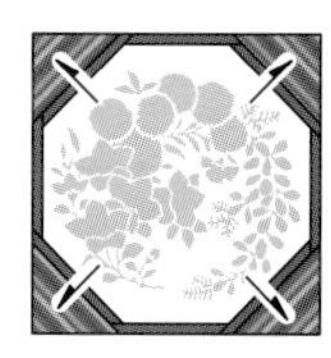

Octagon Block
Make 11.

3. Alternate 2 small-scale print triangle C with 2 navy blue-and-white kite D to make each alternate half block. Sew the halves together, carefully matching points at the center. Press the seam allowances in a clockwise direction.

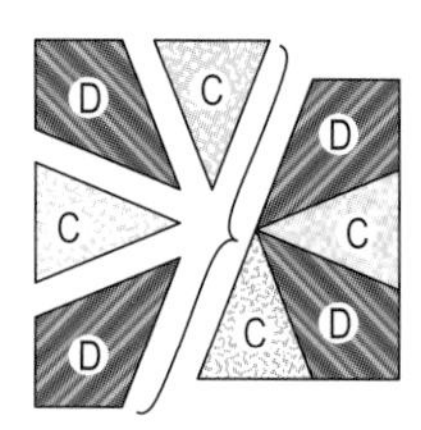

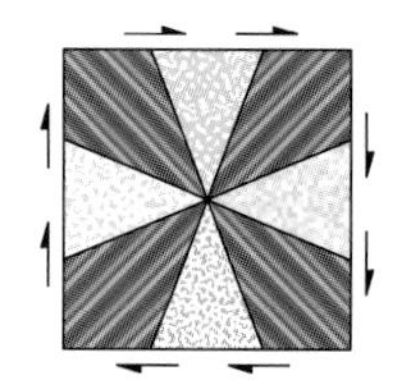

Alternate Block
Make 10.

4. Referring to the diagram, sew the octagon blocks and alternate blocks together in rows. Press the seam allowances in opposite directions from row to row. Sew the rows together.

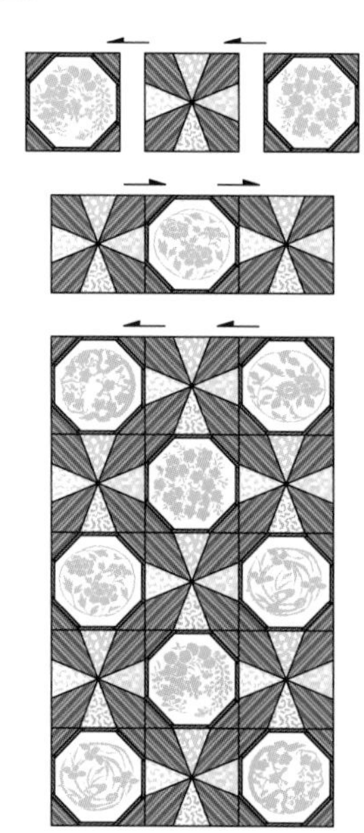

5. To make side block #1, sew a yellow trapezoid F to an orange trapezoid G, then sew a green piece H to F/G, starting and stopping ¼" from the ends of the seam line. Sew a navy blue–and-white stripe triangle E to each end; stop stitching at the G/H seam line. Press seam allowances toward triangle E.

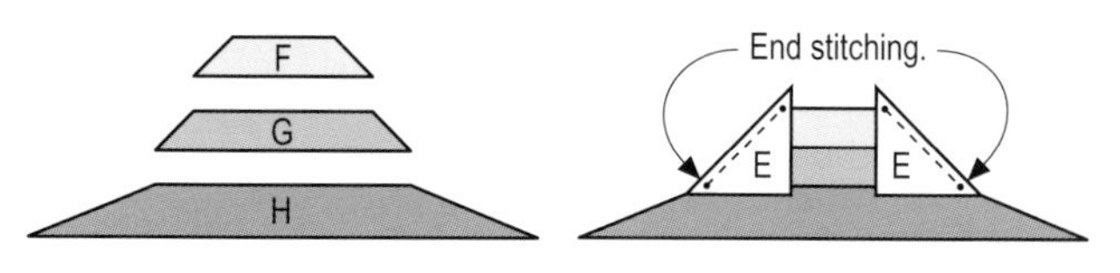

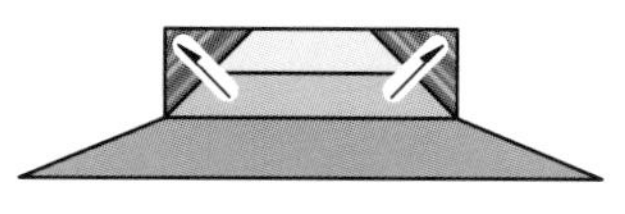

Side Block #1
Make 8.

6. To make side block #2, sew a navy blue–and-white kite D to each long side of a triangle C. Press seam allowances toward kite D.

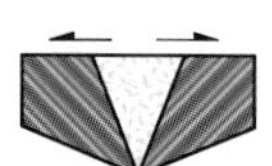

Side Block #2
Make 12.

7. To make a corner block, sew a green piece I to each short side of an orange triangle E, starting and stopping ¼" from the edges. Do not sew the 45°-angle seams yet. Press the seam allowances toward piece I.

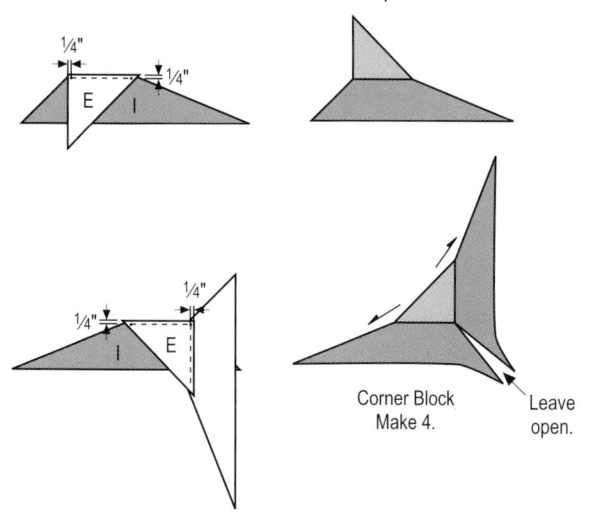

Corner Block
Make 4.

Borders

1. Alternate 4 side block #2 with 3 side block #1. Stitch together to make the side pieced borders.

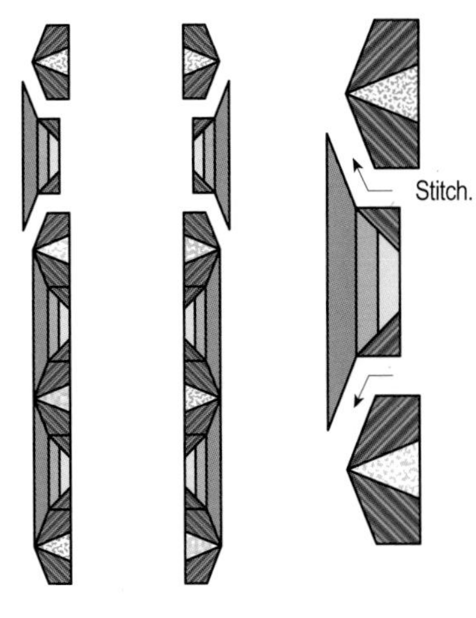

2. Sew a side block #2 to opposite sides of a side block #1 to make the top and bottom pieced borders, then sew a navy blue–and-white triangle E to each end.

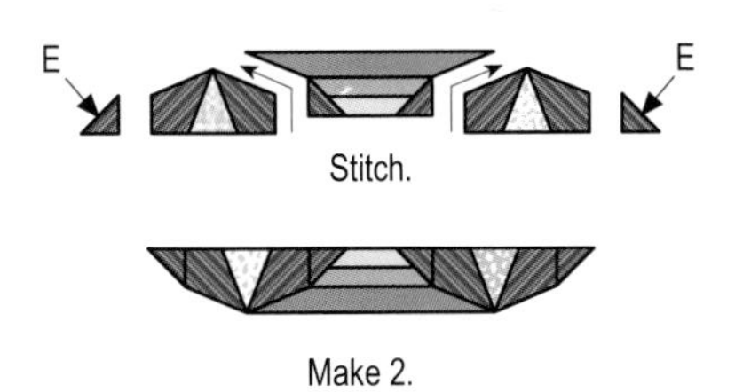

Make 2.

3. Sew the pieced side borders to the quilt top, then add the top and bottom borders.

4. Sew the corner blocks to the quilt, leaving open the seams to be mitered.

5. Join the 5"-wide rust outer border strips in pairs, end to end. Repeat for the 1¾"-wide gray stripe inner border strips.
6. Sew a gray stripe side border strip to each of the rust side, top, and bottom border strips. Press seam allowances toward the rust border.
7. Mark the center of each side of the quilt top and the center of each pieced border. Measure through the center of the quilt top from top to bottom and mark each pieced side border to this measurement. Measure through the center of the quilt top from side to side and mark the pieced top and bottom borders.

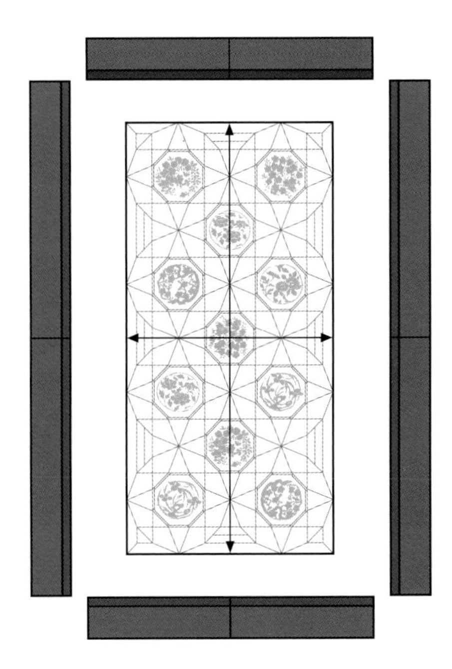

8. Pin, matching marks, then stitch the borders to the quilt top, beginning and ending ¼" from the corners. Press seam allowances toward borders.

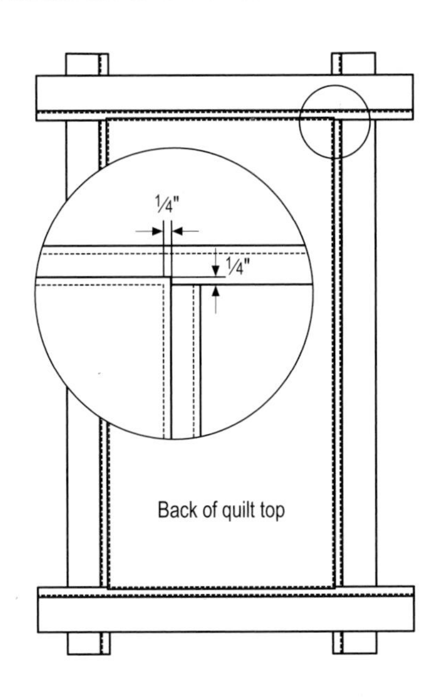

9. Miter the corners, treating the corner piece I, the gray stripe, and the rust borders as one strip. Trim the ends, then press the seam open.

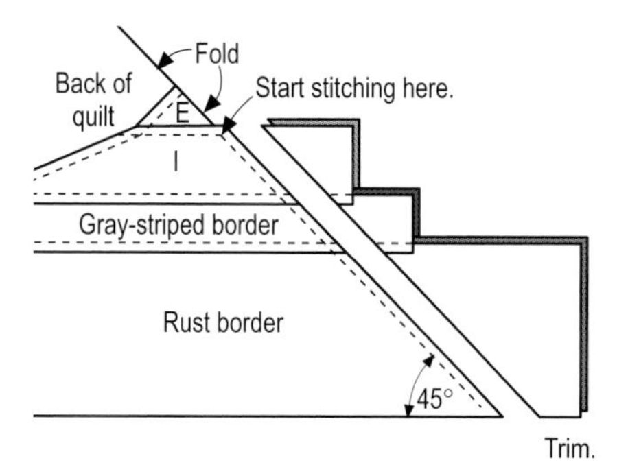

Finishing

1. From the floral and butterfly print fabrics, cut out flowers and butterflies, leaving a ¼"-wide seam allowance around the edges. Using your favorite method, appliqué the pieces to the quilt top in a pleasing arrangement.
2. Layer the quilt top with batting and backing; baste.
3. Quilt as desired.
4. Bind the edges with the gray stripe strips.

Note: Youko Morita chose an extra-wide binding for "*Bingatazome*." She centered the stripes in the fabric and mitered the corners, giving the appearance of a frame.

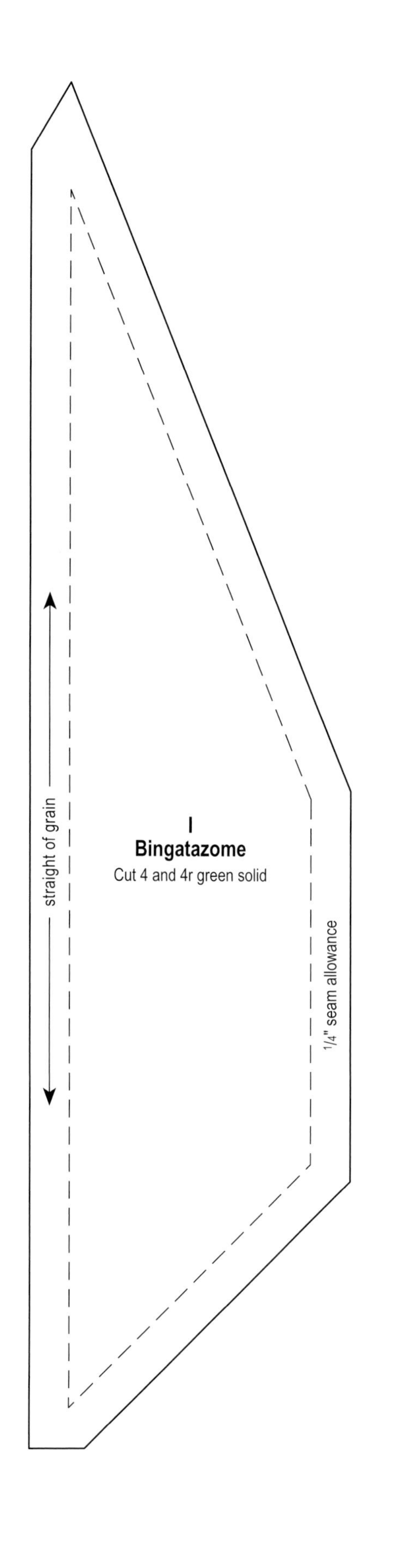

C
Bingatazome
Cut 52 assorted prints

D
Bingatazome
Cut 64 navy blue stripe

straight of grain

H
Bingatazome
Cut 8 green solid

1/4" seam allowance

Place on fold.

F
Bingatazome
Cut 8 yellow solid

G
Bingatazome
Cut 8 orange solid

E
Bingatazome
Cut 64 navy blue stripe
Cut 4 orange solid

Hinamatsuri *(Girl's Day)*

Finished quilt size: 22" x 28"

On Girl's Day, March 3, people adorn their homes with colorful dolls, peach blossoms, brightly colored candies, and painted paper lanterns. It's a fantastic event, following a tradition of more than three hundred years. Despite minor regional differences, this exciting event is still going strong even in modern Japan. Lately, due to the high price of decorations and the lack of space, simple sets and homemade items like this quilt have become increasingly popular.

The designs in the upper left and lower right corners are called kumoi. *The image is derived from clouds, or* kumo, *in Japanese and is frequently used in Japanese art and* kimono *designs.*

Materials: 44"-wide fabric

5/8 yd. white-on-white print for background
3/8 yd. brown print for border and binding
Scraps of assorted cotton fabrics for appliquéd *kumoi* designs and each figure's *kimono*, sash, face, hair, hat, and trim
1 rectangle, 25" x 32", for backing
2 heavy strings or cords, each 10" long, 1 yellow and 1 green
Black and red embroidery floss for eyes and mouths
25" x 32" piece of batting

Cutting

Cut all strips across the width of the fabric from selvage to selvage unless otherwise noted.

From the white-on-white print, cut:
1 rectangle, 18½" x 24½", for background

From the brown print, cut:
2 strips, each 2½" x 32", for borders
2 strips, each 2½" x 26", for borders
3 strips, each 1" wide, for binding

From the backing fabric, cut:
1 rectangle, 26" x 32"

Assembly

1. Trace the patterns for appliqué, referring to the placement diagram on the pullout. Cut 1 of each piece for the figures, adding a scant ¼"-wide seam allowance. Cut 2 of each *kumoi* piece. Prepare all pieces for appliqué, using your favorite method.
2. Referring to the placement diagram, appliqué *kumoi* pieces #1–#3 to the upper and lower corners of the background.
3. For the male figure on the right, appliqué pieces #4–#14. Cut the green cord in half and secure to the figure's hair as shown so the hat (piece #15) will cover the ends. Appliqué the hat.

4. For the female figure on the left, appliqué pieces #16–#19.
5. From 2 different fabrics, cut 1 strip, each ¾" x 14½". Fold each strip in half lengthwise. Cut each strip into 2 segments, one 3¾" long and one 10¾" long for *kimono* layers.

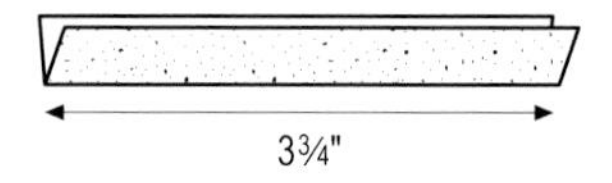

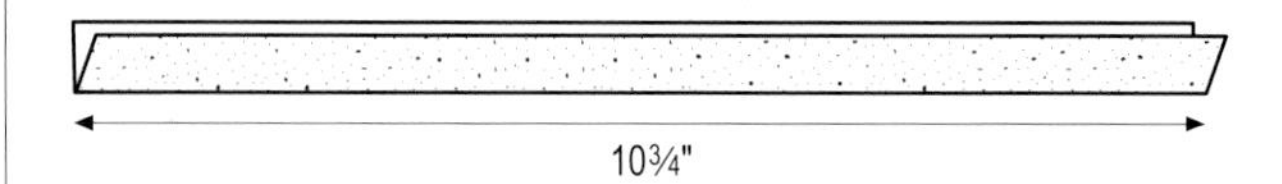

6. Lay one 3¾"-long strip on top of the other, so the folded edge of the top strip is ⅛" from the folded edge of the bottom strip. Baste the strips together to make short strip units. Repeat for the 10¾" strips to make long strip units.

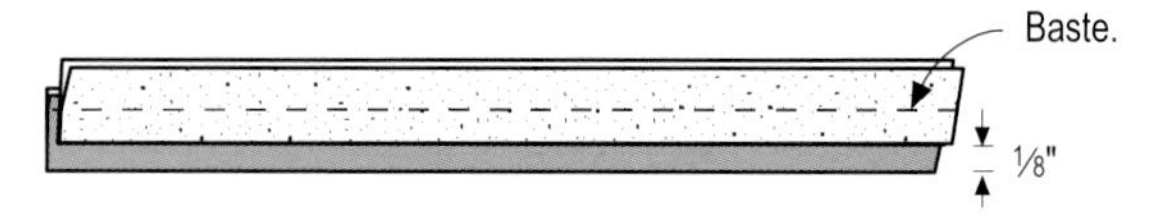

7. Turn under a ¼"-wide seam allowance along the lower edge of piece #20. Turn under ¼" of the left end of the short strip unit and baste to the hem of piece #20. Appliqué piece #20 to the background, appliquéing the lower edge along the hem of the *kimono* through all layers. Appliqué the left edge of the folded strips to the background, but leave the lower edges free.

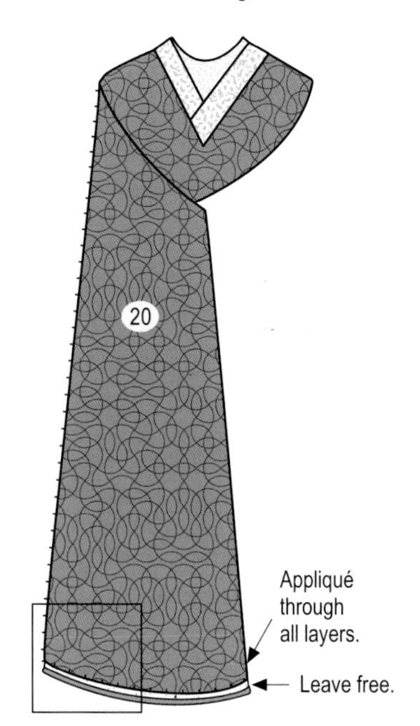

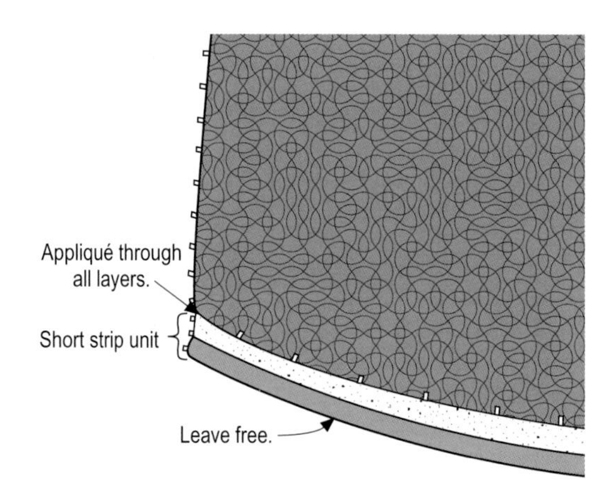

8. Turn under the left and lower edges of piece #21. Baste the long folded strip unit to piece #21 the way you did in step 7, mitering the corner and turning under the raw ends of the strip. Appliqué piece #21 through all layers, leaving the lower edges of the folded strips free.

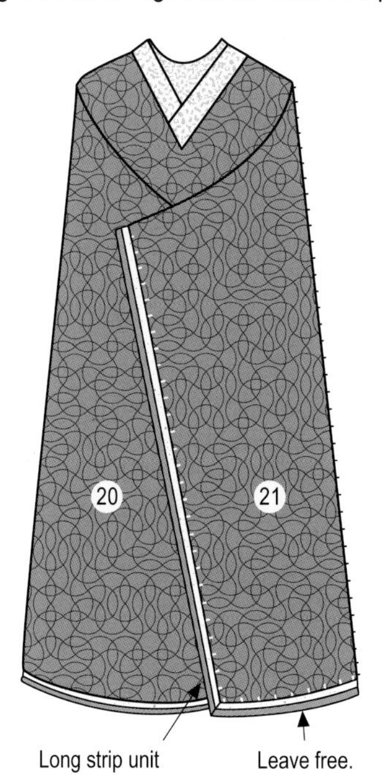

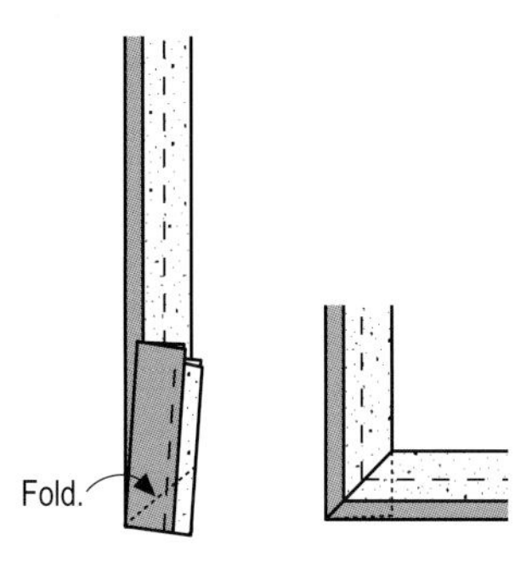

9. Referring to the pullout, appliqué pieces #22–#24. Cut the yellow cord in half and secure to the figure's head the way you did in step 3 so the hat will cover the ends of the cords. Appliqué the hat (piece #25).
10. Tie the cords in bows under the figures' chins. Stitch to secure if necessary.

Border

Sew the 2½" x 32" and the 2½" x 26" border strips to the side and top and bottom edges of the quilt top, mitering the corners. Trim the seam allowances to ¼"; press open.

Finishing

1. For each face, take a long and short running stitch as shown for the eyes and mouth. Use black embroidery floss for the eyes and red for the mouth.

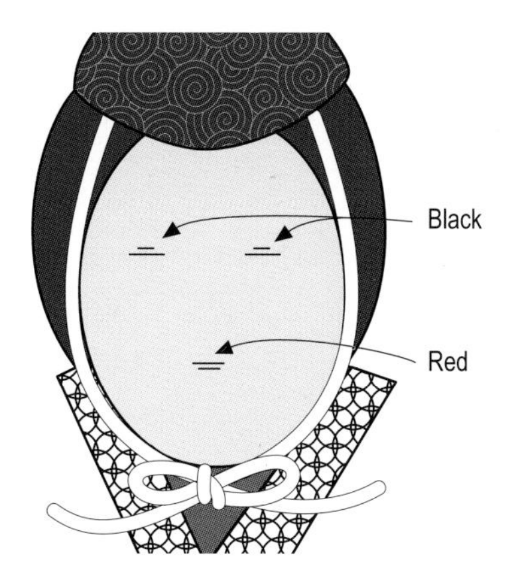

2. Layer the quilt top with backing and batting; baste.
3. Quilt as desired.
4. Bind the edges.

Harukaze ni Notte *(Ride the Spring Breeze)*

Finished quilt size: 75" x 75"

Finished block sizes

Log Cabin: 6¼" x 6¼"

Flower: 7" x 7"

Corner Block

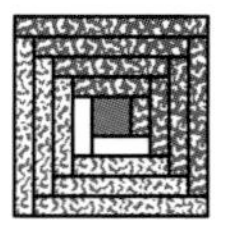

Log Cabin Block

All people think of their hometown or country as being beautiful. I feel the same way about Japan, especially during the long and beautiful springtime. Although it is still very cold, the plum trees begin to bloom in late February—a kind of early spring—and it makes me happy to think that spring is just around the corner.

Then, when the cherry trees begin to bloom, everyone finds it hard to stay home. People go out to view the cherry blossoms, not only during the day, but also at night. Under the trees, they eat and drink and have a good time.

Next, the azalea and dogwood bloom, and the flower shops display many different kinds of flowers. When the hydrangeas bloom during the rainy season, we spend the time blessed with beautiful greenery and flowers, and enjoy the fragrant springtime breeze.

Flower Block

Materials: 44"-wide fabric

¾ yd. *total* assorted light green small-scale prints for Log Cabin blocks (Fabric A)
½ yd. light green plaid for Log Cabin blocks (Fabric B)
1 yd. medium green print #1 for Log Cabin blocks (Fabric C)
1⅞ yds. medium green print #2 for Log Cabin blocks (Fabric D)
1¼ yds. medium–dark green print for Log Cabin blocks (Fabric E)
1 yd. dark green print for Log Cabin blocks and binding (Fabric F)
1½ yds. off-white solid for Flower blocks (Fabric G)
1½ yds. *total* light and medium green solids for Flower blocks (Fabric H)
½ yd. *total* assorted medium–dark green solids for Log Cabin center squares (Fabric I)
Assorted scraps of pink, red, brown, blue, purple, and yellow solids and floral prints for Flower blocks
4½ yds. for backing
85" x 85" piece of batting

Cutting

Cut the number of strips required from each fabric. Cut all strips across the width of the fabric from selvage to selvage unless otherwise noted.

Fabric	No. of Strips	Strip Width	No. of Squares	Dimensions
A	13	1⅛"		
B	13	1⅛"		
C	24	1⅛"		
D	52	1⅛"	4	1⅛" x 1⅛"
E	31	1⅛"	4	1⅛" x 1⅛"
F	9	1⅛"	40	1⅛" x 1⅛"
	8	1"*		
G	43	1⅛"		
H	43	1⅛"**		
I	6	1¾"	140	1¾" x 1¾"

* Cut these strips for binding.
** Use the remaining fabric H and the assorted scraps for the Flower blocks.

Block Assembly

Log Cabin Blocks

Note: As you make the Log Cabin blocks, refer to the piecing diagram below for dimensions (measurements include seam allowances). The illustrations on page 26 show the required fabrics for each block. Use darker-value fabric for Log Cabin segments #1, #4, #5, #8, #9, #12, #13, and #16. Use light-value fabric for segments #2, #3, #6, #7, #10, #11, #14, and #15.

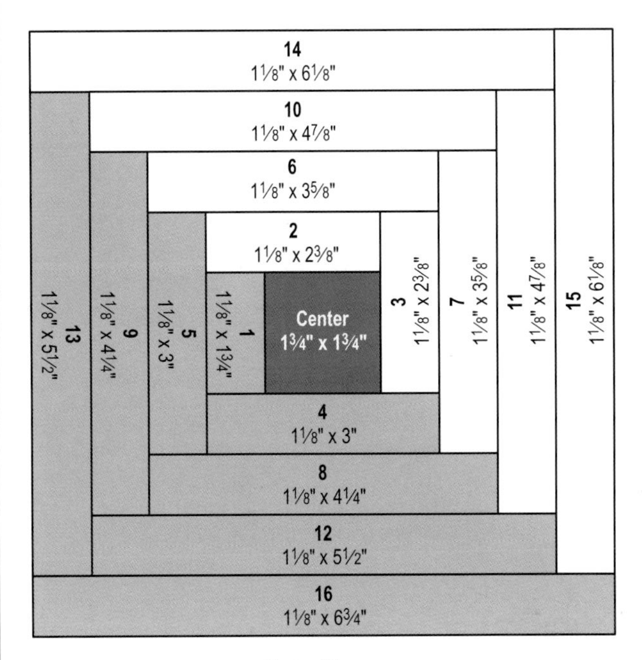

Piecing Diagram
Log Cabin Block

1. Starting with a 1¾" fabric I center square, assemble each Log Cabin block and side block, following the piecing diagram for segments #1–#7.

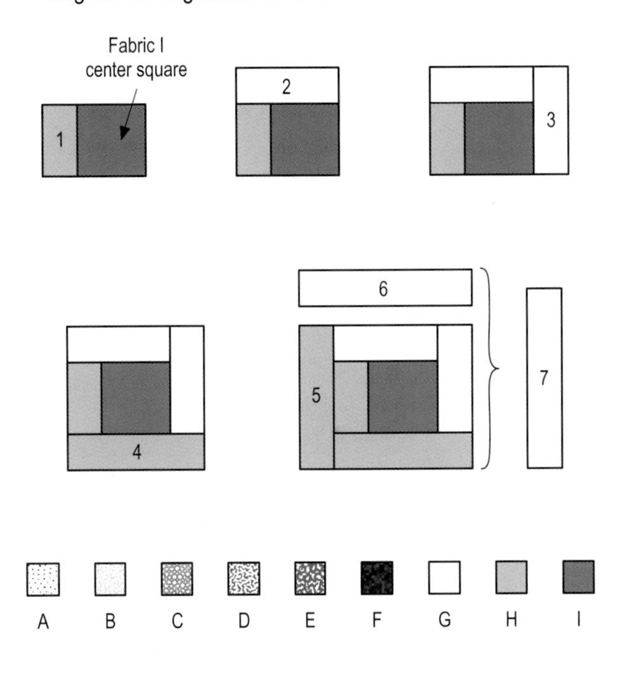

Continue sewing segments #8–#16 to the block in a clockwise direction. Refer to the illustrations for the correct fabrics and number of blocks. Label each block with its number.

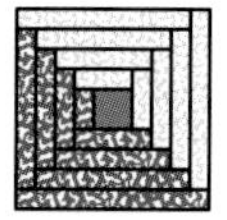
Block 2
Make 4.

Block 4
Make 4.

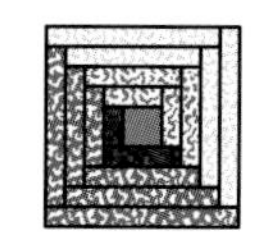
Block 6
Make 4.

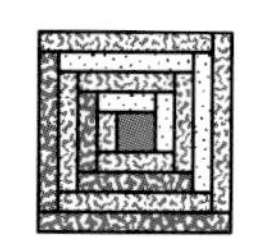
Block 10
Make 4.

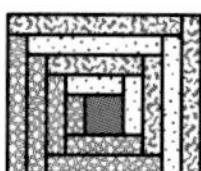
Block 16
Make 4.

Block 20
Make 4.

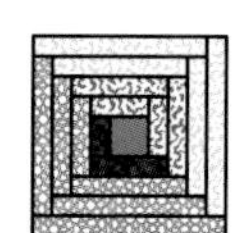
Block 22
Make 4.

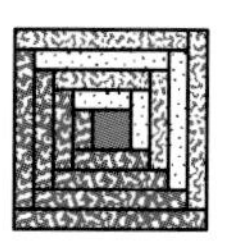
Block 24
Make 4.

Blocks 12 and 14
Make 4.

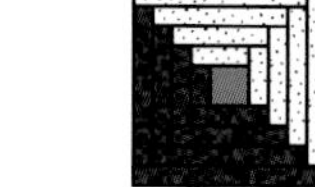
Blocks 8 and 18
Make 4.

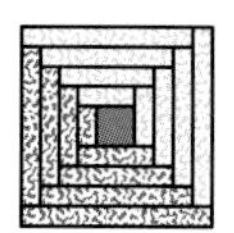
Blocks 8 and 18
Make 4.

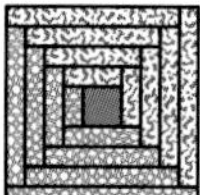
Side Blocks T2, T4, B2, B4, R2, R4, L2, L4
Make 16.

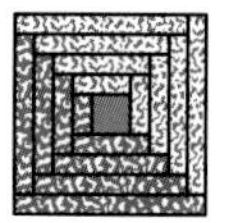
Blocks 12 and 14, Side Blocks T1, T3, T5, B1, B3, B5, R1, R3, R5, L1, L3, L5
Make 28.

2. Sew the Log Cabin blocks together in groups of 4 to make blocks #2, #4, #6, #10, #16, #20, #22, and #24. Refer to the photo on page 24 for color arrangement.

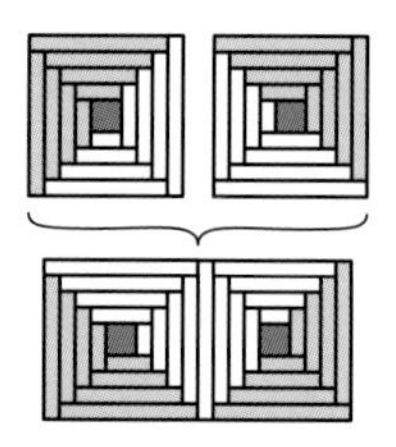

3. Assemble side blocks T1–5, L1–5, R1–5, and B1–5, joining the Log Cabin blocks along the dark edges.

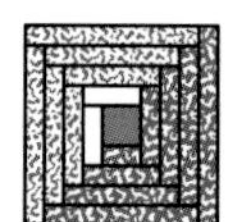

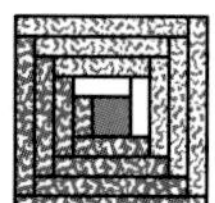

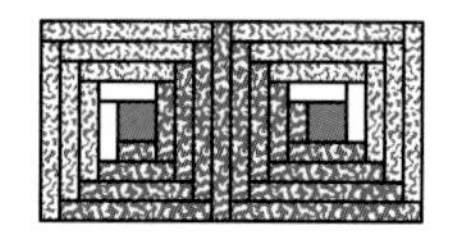

Corner Blocks

1. Cut each segment, following the dimensions given on the piecing diagram (measurements include seam allowances). Sew a 1⅛" fabric F square to each 1⅛" fabric D and fabric E square. Sew an F/D unit to an F/E unit to make the pieced center square. Sew a fabric F square to each fabric D segment.

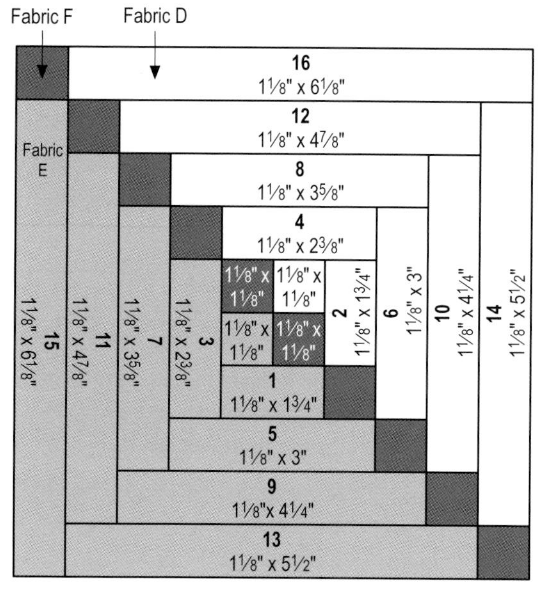

Piecing Diagram
Corner Block

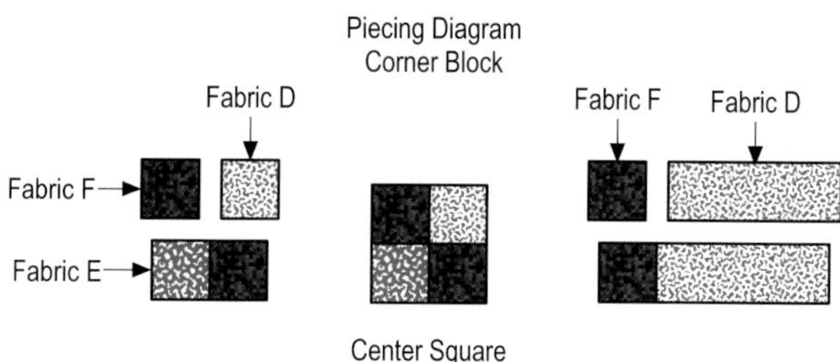

Center Square
Make 4.

2. Assemble the block, following the piecing order. Press the seam allowances toward the edges.

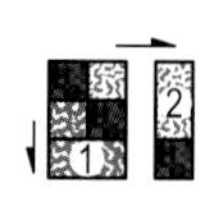

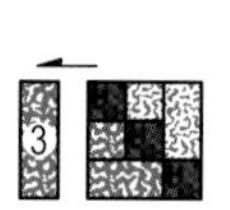

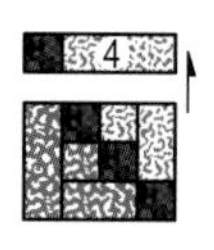

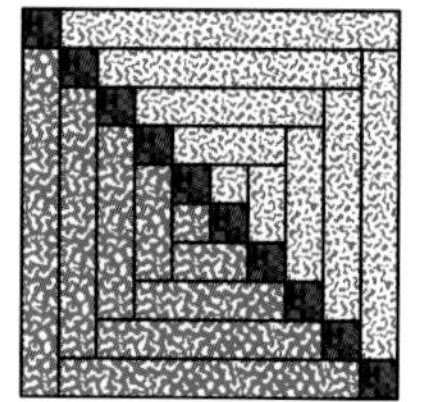
Corner Block
Make 4.

Log Cabin Background Blocks

Starting with a fabric I center square, assemble 52 Log Cabin blocks, using fabrics G and H. Refer to the measurements given in step 1 of "Log Cabin Blocks" for cutting each piece.

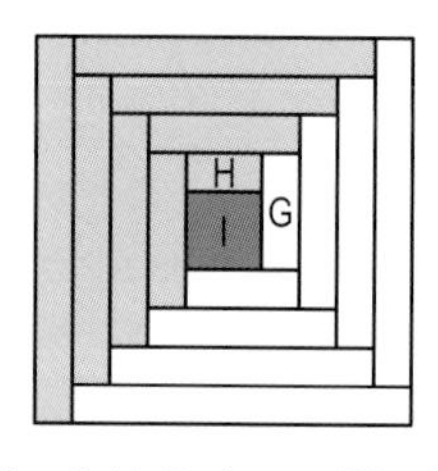

Log Cabin Background Block
Make 52.

Note: For those who are hand piecing, do not piece the entire portion of the off-white section. For the fabric G segments, cut segments #2 and #3 according to the dimensions given on page 25. Substitute 1⅛" x 3" segments for each remaining fabric G segment. The Flower block covers this corner of the block.

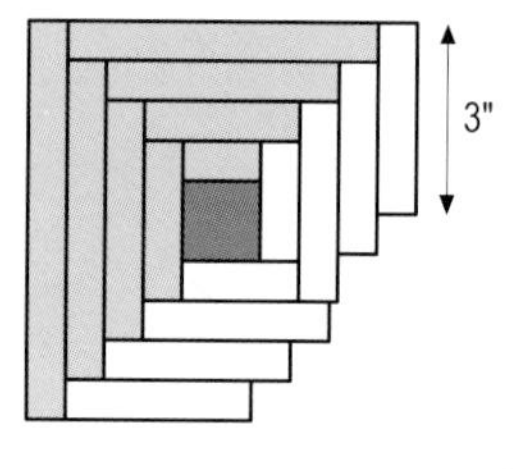

Flower Blocks

Assemble the 3½" x 3½" Flower block quadrants, using assorted fabric scraps for the flowers and leaves. Use fabric H for the block backgrounds.

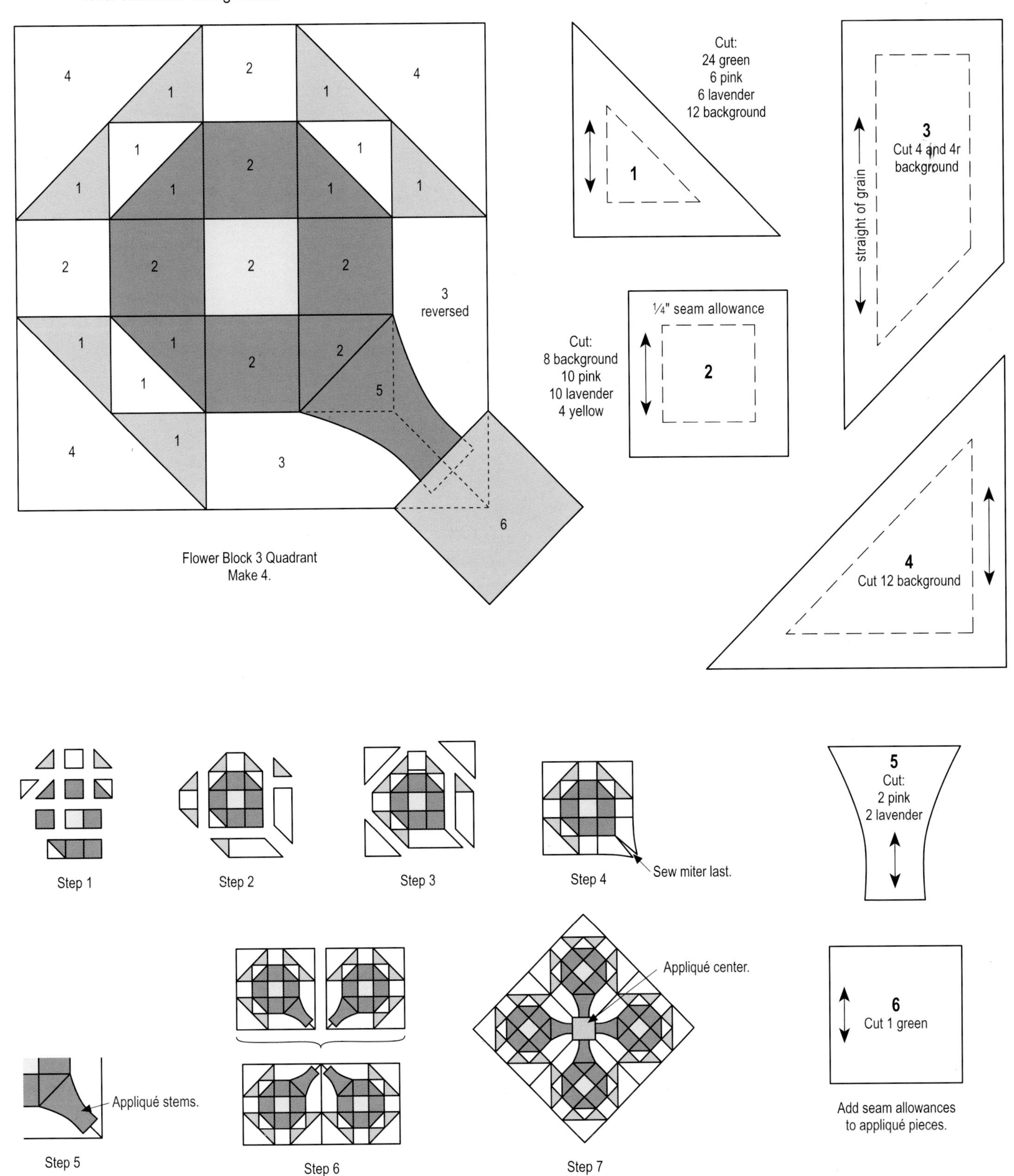

Flower Block 3 Quadrant
Make 4.

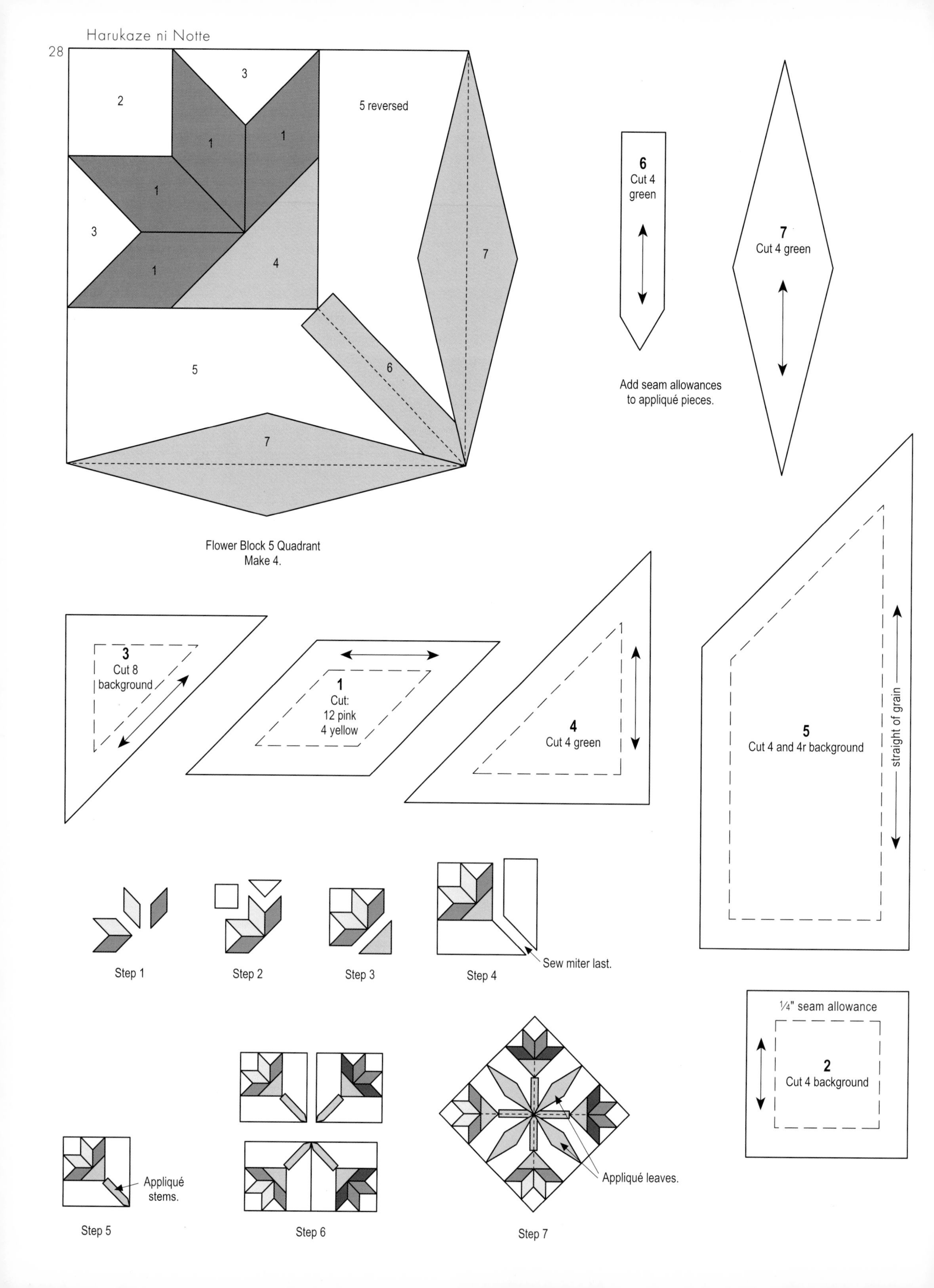

Flower Block 5 Quadrant
Make 4.

Step 1 Step 2 Step 3 Step 4

Step 5 Step 6 Step 7

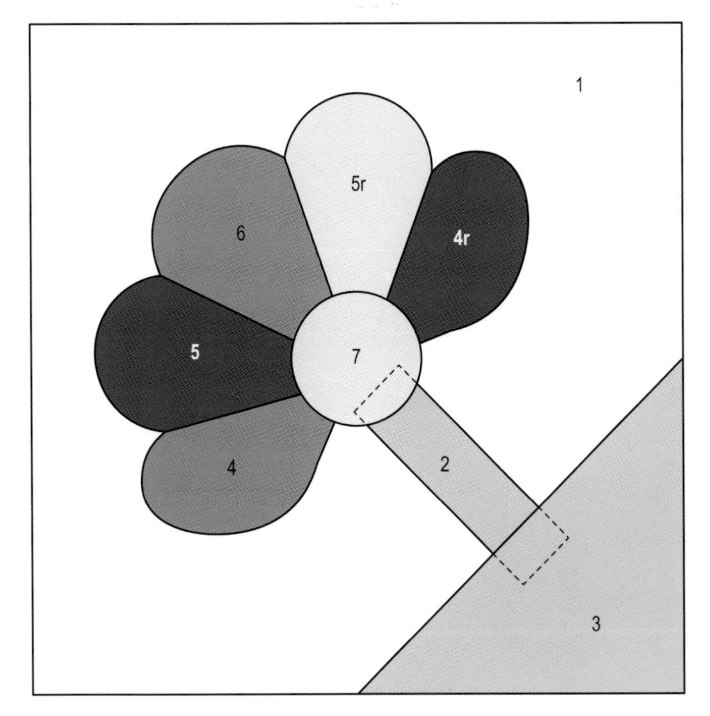

Flower Block 7 Quadrant
Make 4.

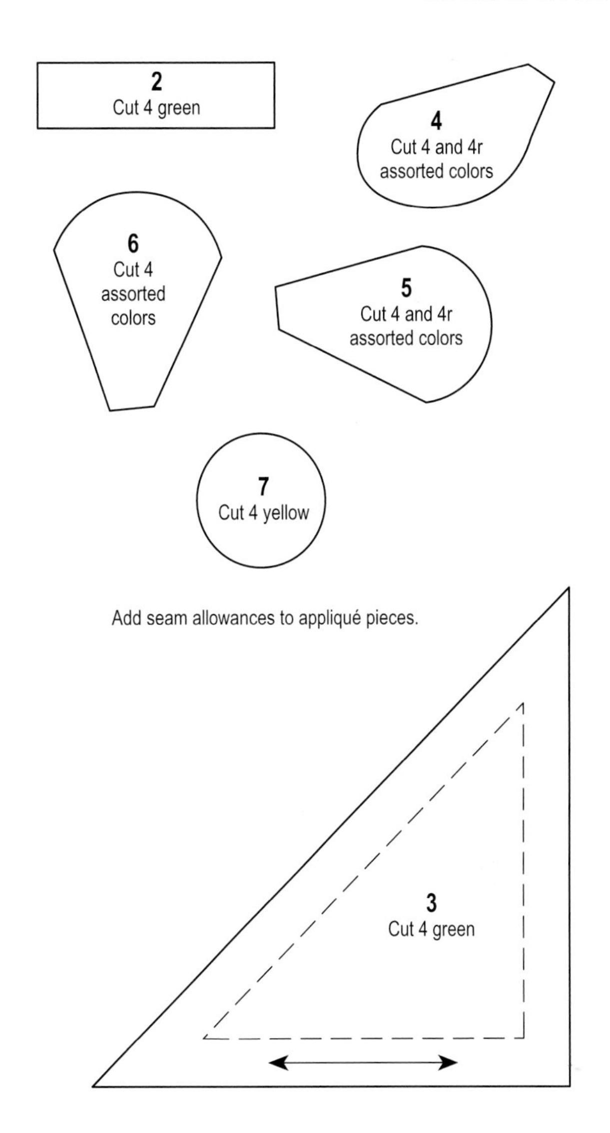

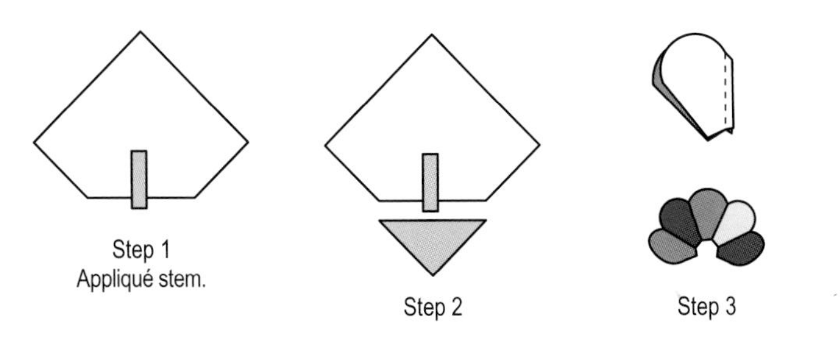

Step 1
Appliqué stem.

Step 2

Step 3

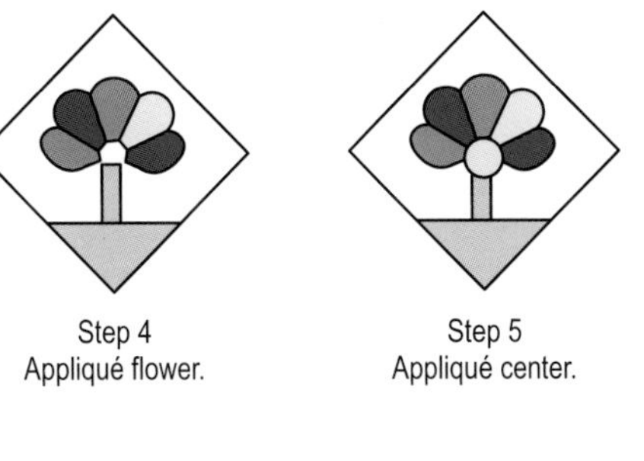

Step 4
Appliqué flower.

Step 5
Appliqué center.

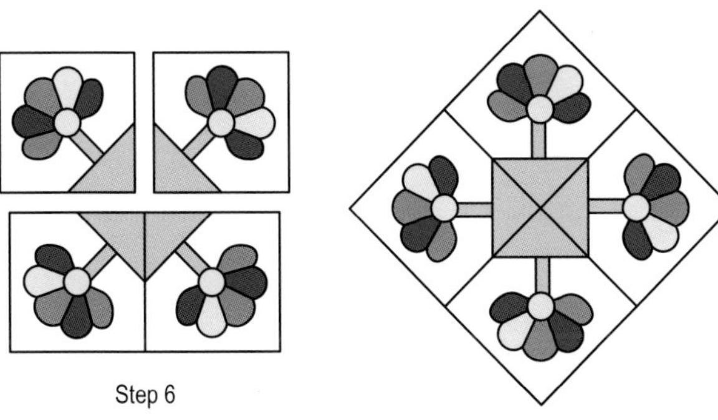

Step 6

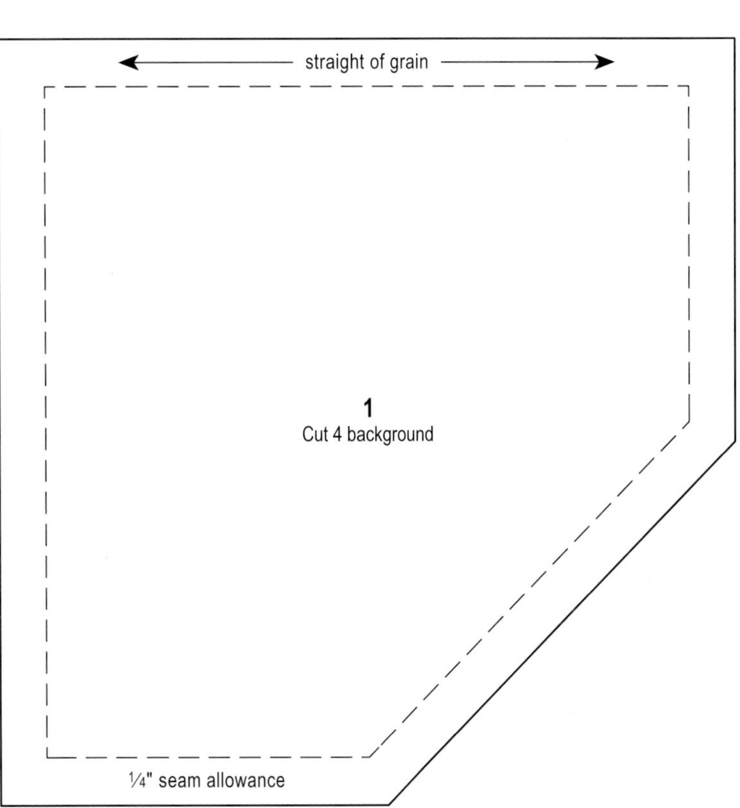

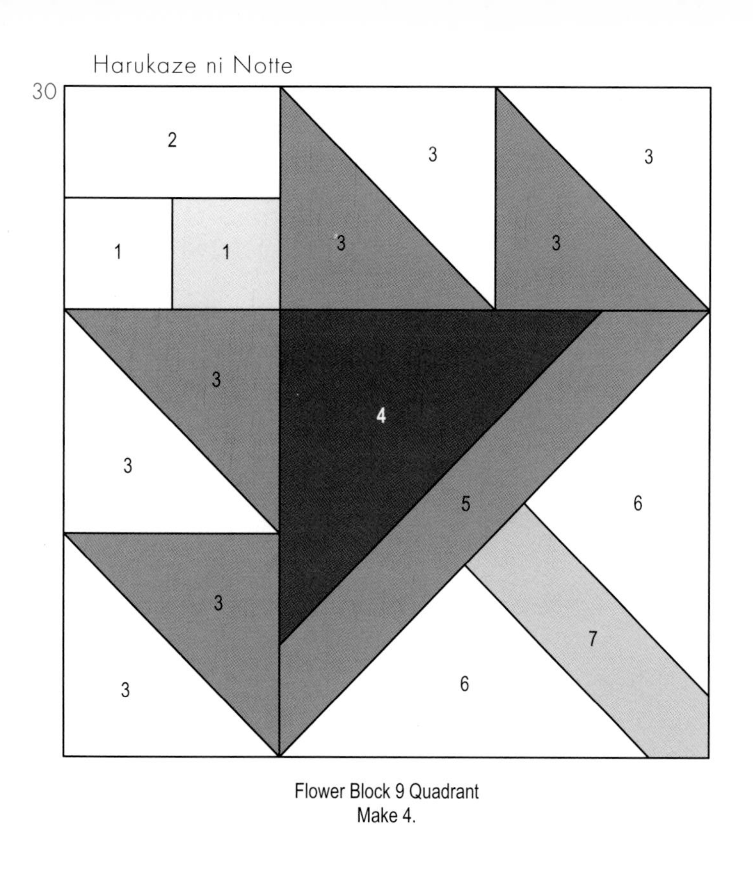

Flower Block 9 Quadrant
Make 4.

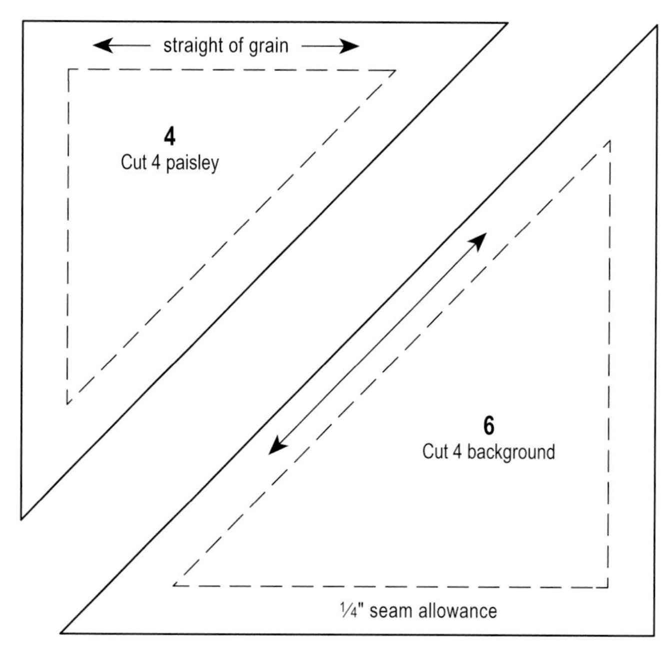

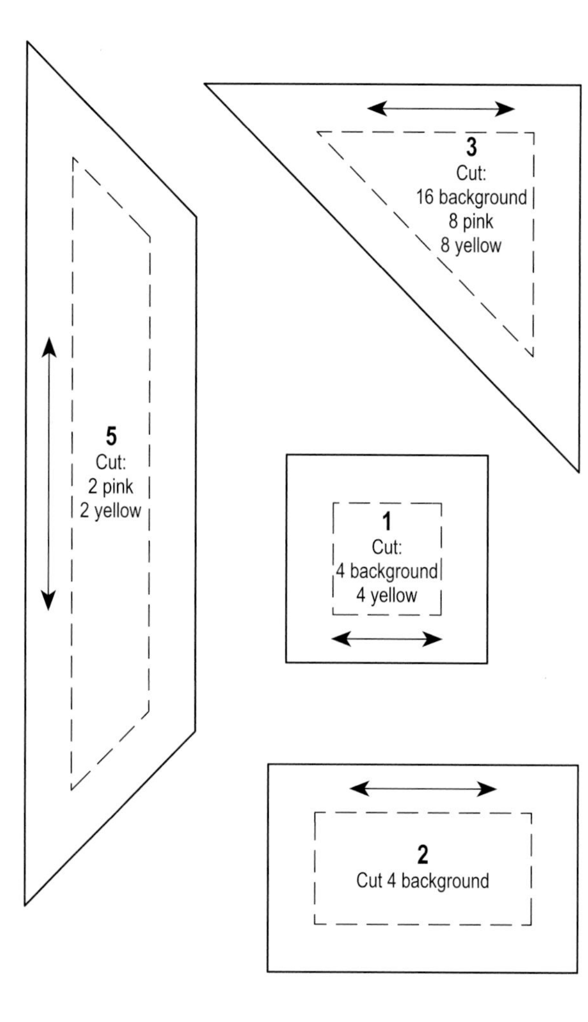

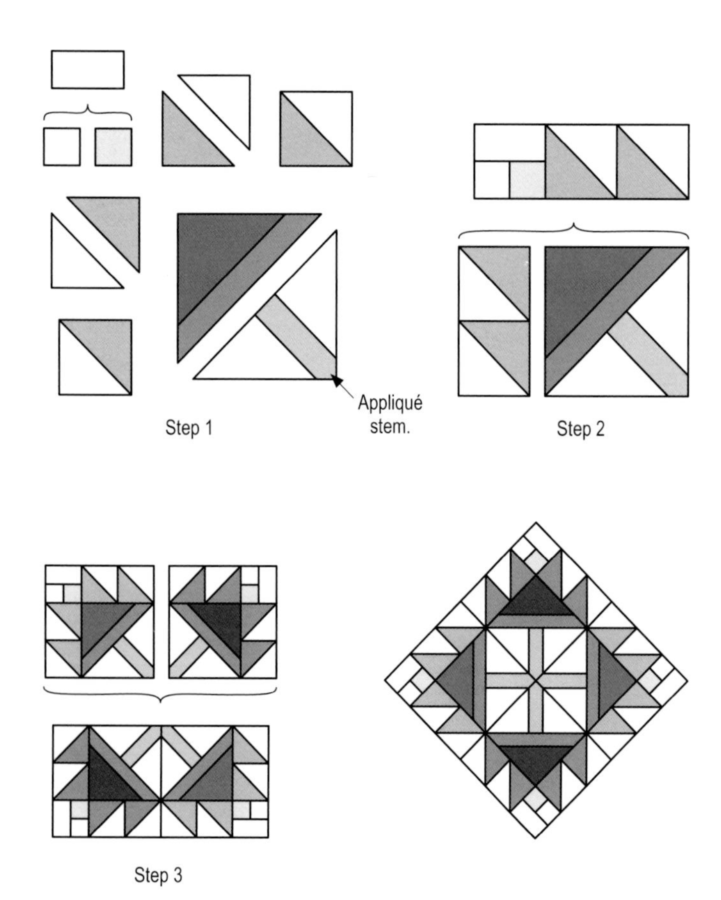

Step 1

Step 2

Step 3

7
Cut 4 green

Add seam allowance to appliqué piece.

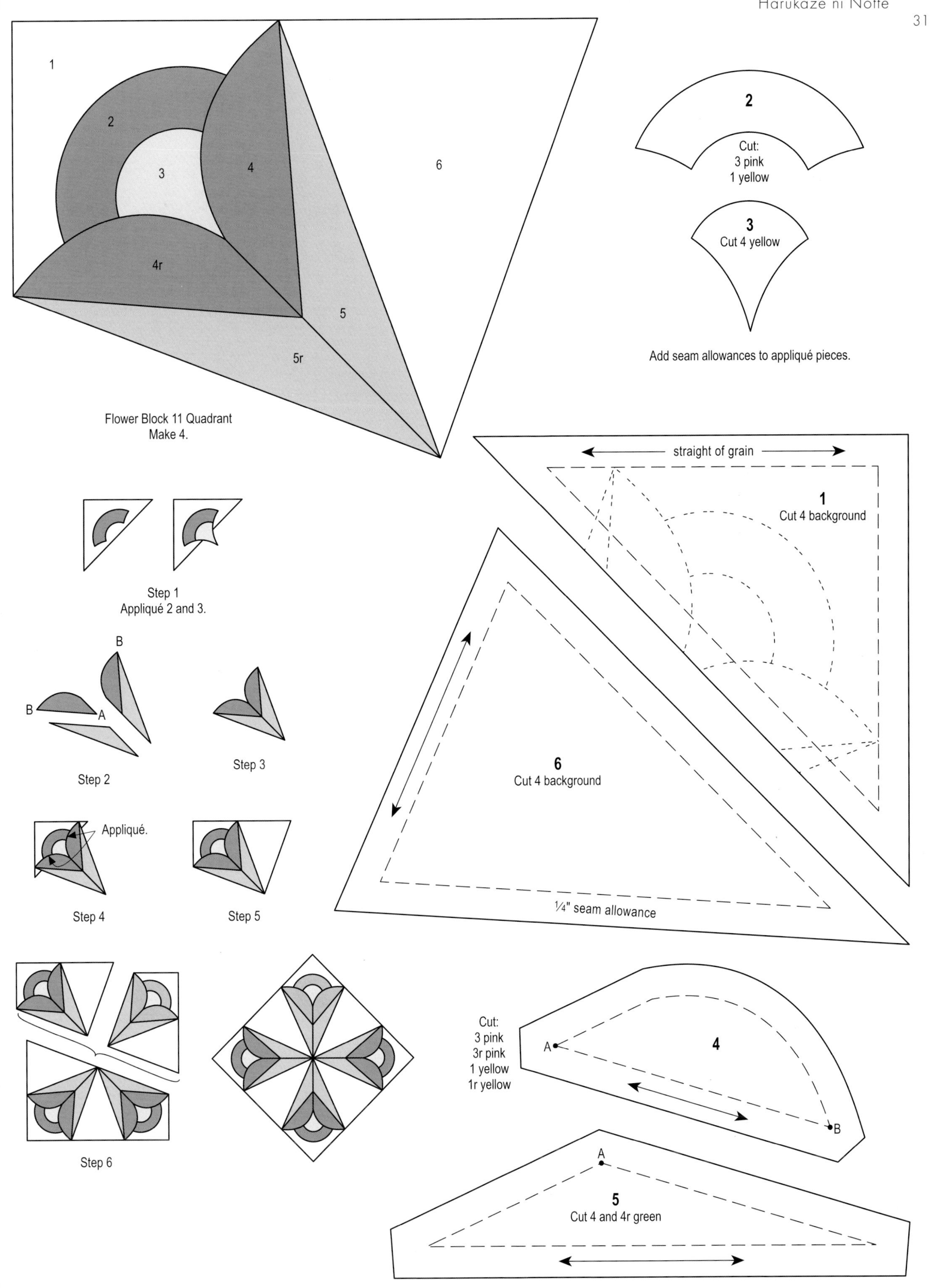
1
2
3
4
4r
5
5r
6
Flower Block 11 Quadrant
Make 4.
2
Cut:
3 pink
1 yellow
3
Cut 4 yellow
Add seam allowances to appliqué pieces.
straight of grain
1
Cut 4 background
6
Cut 4 background
¼" seam allowance
Step 1
Appliqué 2 and 3.
B
B
A
Step 2
Step 3
Appliqué.
Step 4
Step 5
Step 6
Cut:
3 pink
3r pink
1 yellow
1r yellow
A
4
B
A
5
Cut 4 and 4r green

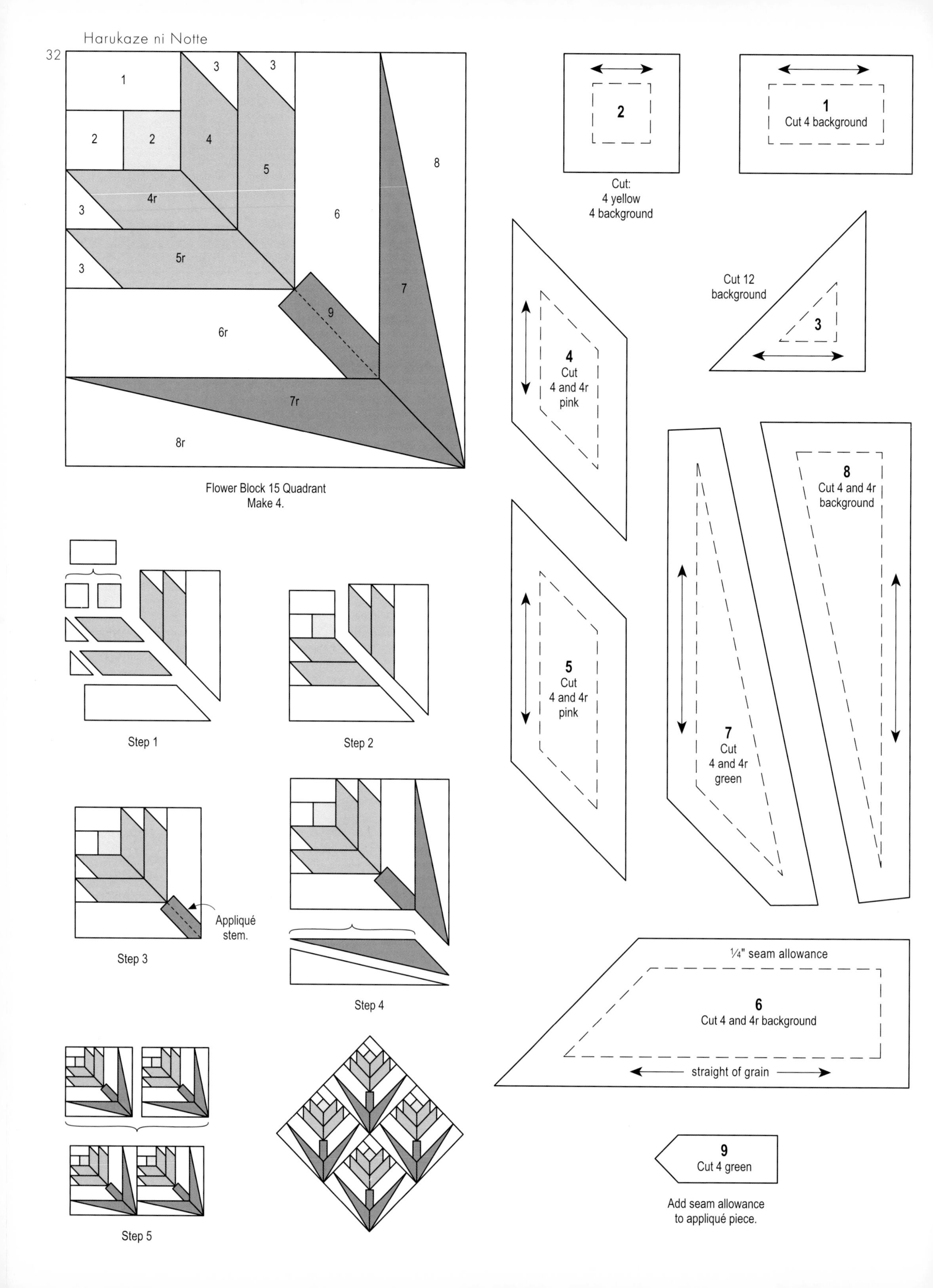
1
2
2
3
3
4
5
4r
3
3
5r
6
8
7
9
6r
7r
8r
Flower Block 15 Quadrant
Make 4.
2
Cut:
4 yellow
4 background
1
Cut 4 background
Cut 12
background
3
4
Cut
4 and 4r
pink
5
Cut
4 and 4r
pink
7
Cut
4 and 4r
green
8
Cut 4 and 4r
background
Step 1
Step 2
Step 3
Appliqué
stem.
Step 4
Step 5
¼" seam allowance
6
Cut 4 and 4r background
straight of grain
9
Cut 4 green
Add seam allowance
to appliqué piece.

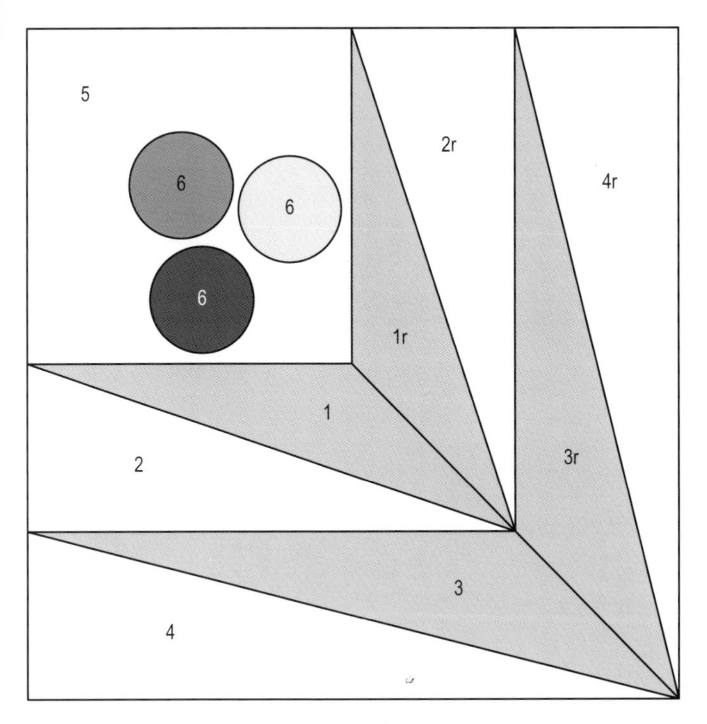

Flower Block 17 Quadrant
Make 4.

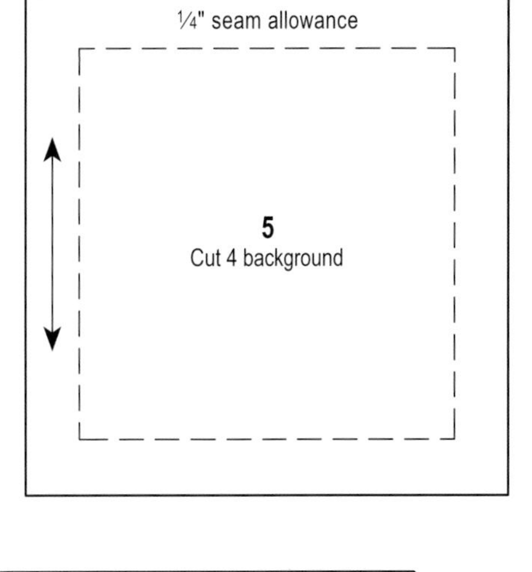

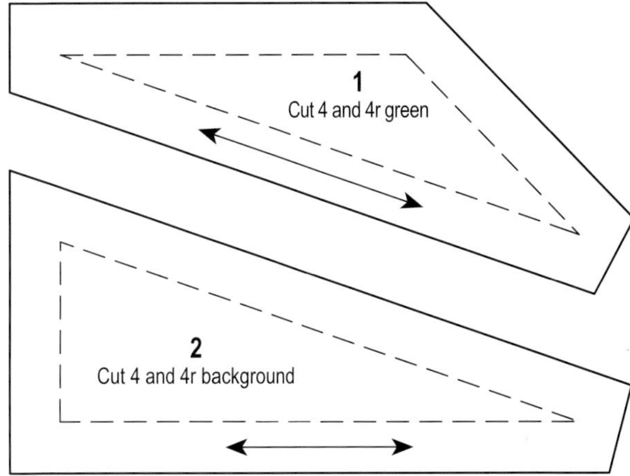

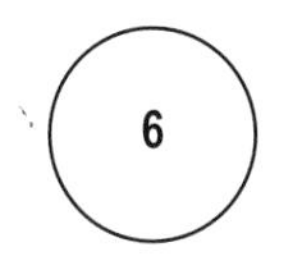

Cut 12 assorted colors
Add seam allowance to appliqué piece.

3
Cut 4 and 4r green

4
Cut 4 and 4r background

straight of grain

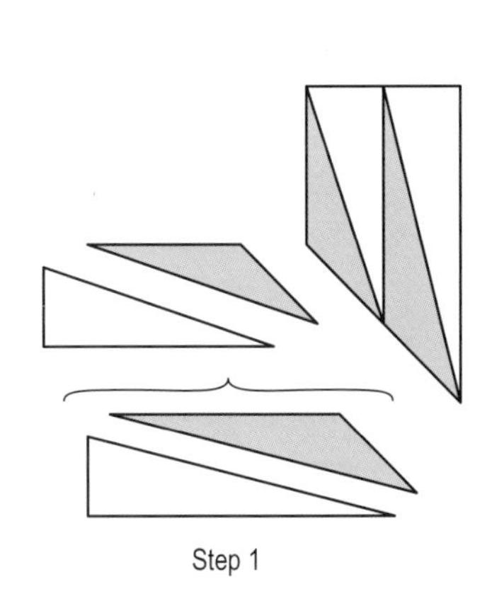

Step 1

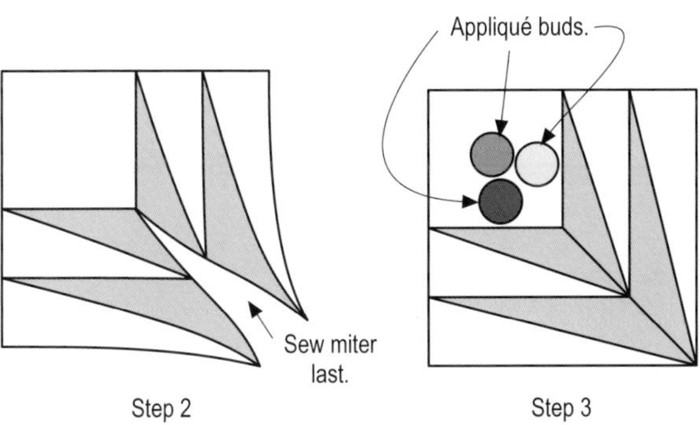

Step 2

Step 3

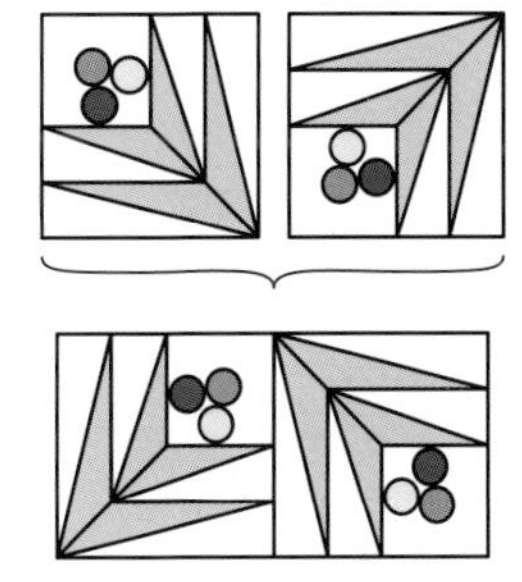

Step 4

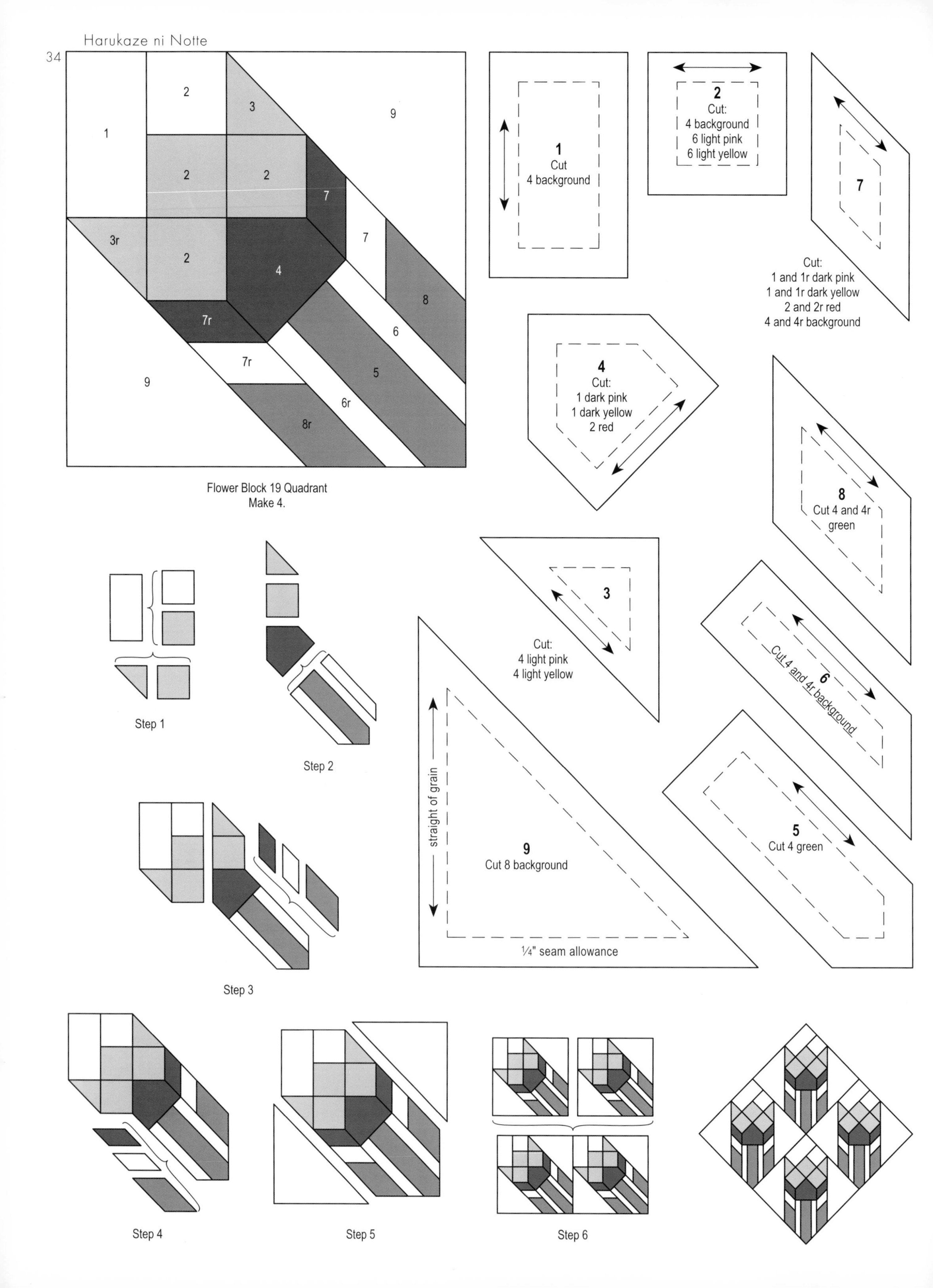
1
2
3
9
2
2
7
3r
2
7
4
8
7r
6
7r
9
5
6r
8r
Flower Block 19 Quadrant
Make 4.
1
Cut
4 background
2
Cut:
4 background
6 light pink
6 light yellow
7
Cut:
1 and 1r dark pink
1 and 1r dark yellow
2 and 2r red
4 and 4r background
4
Cut:
1 dark pink
1 dark yellow
2 red
8
Cut 4 and 4r
green
3
Cut:
4 light pink
4 light yellow
6
Cut 4 and 4r background
5
Cut 4 green
straight of grain
9
Cut 8 background
¼" seam allowance
Step 1
Step 2
Step 3
Step 4
Step 5
Step 6

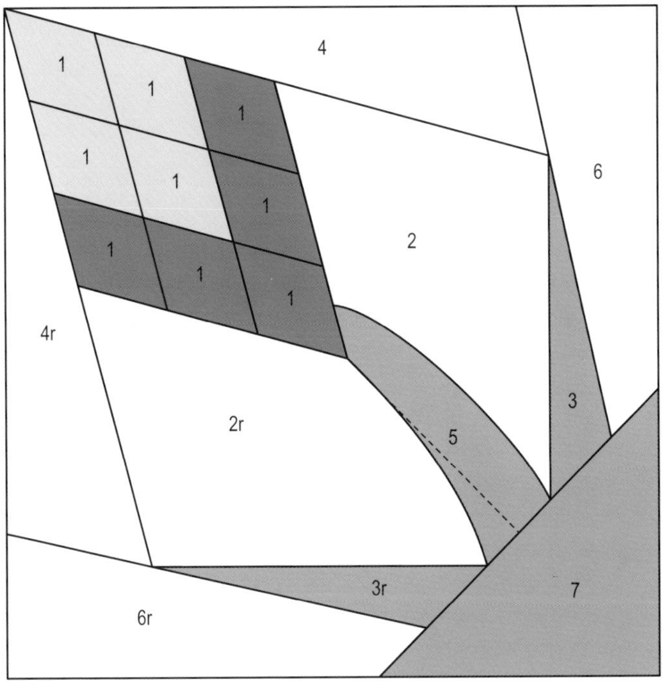

1 1 1 1 1 1 1 1 1
4
4r
2
2r
3
3r
5
6
6r
7

Flower Block 21 Quadrant
Make 4.

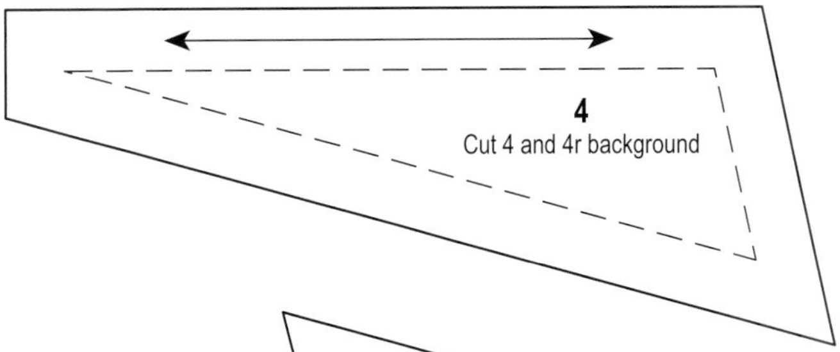

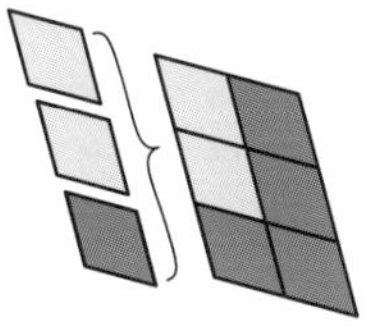

Step 1

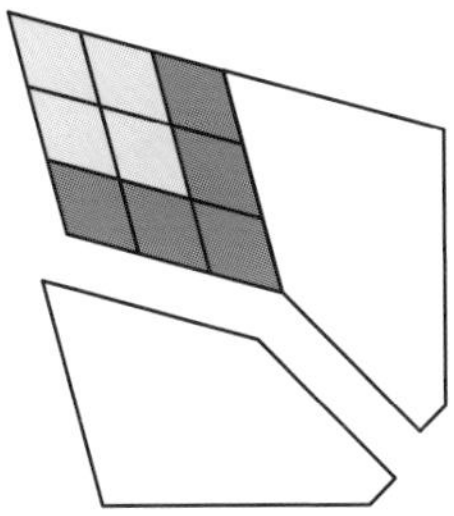

Step 2

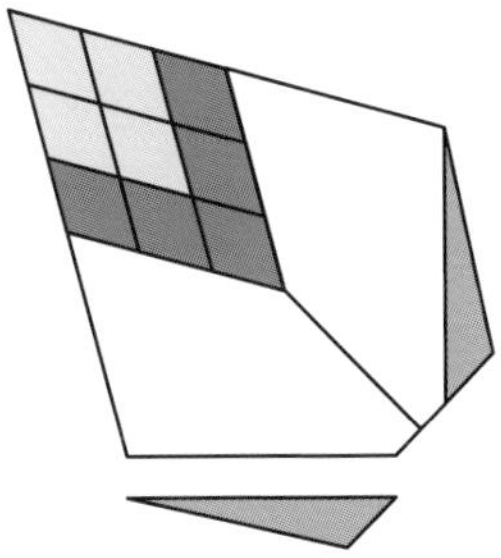

Step 3

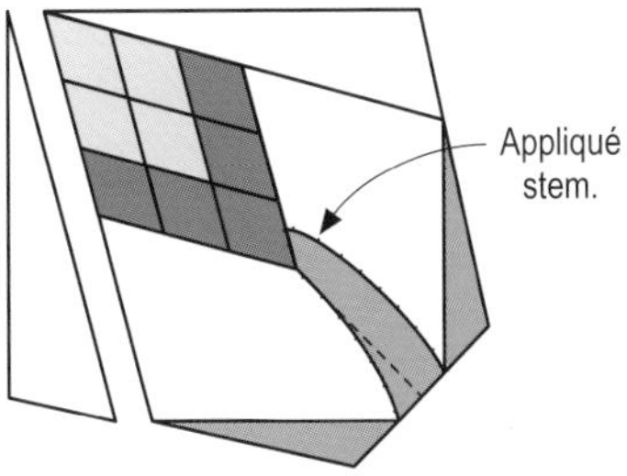

Appliqué stem.

Step 4

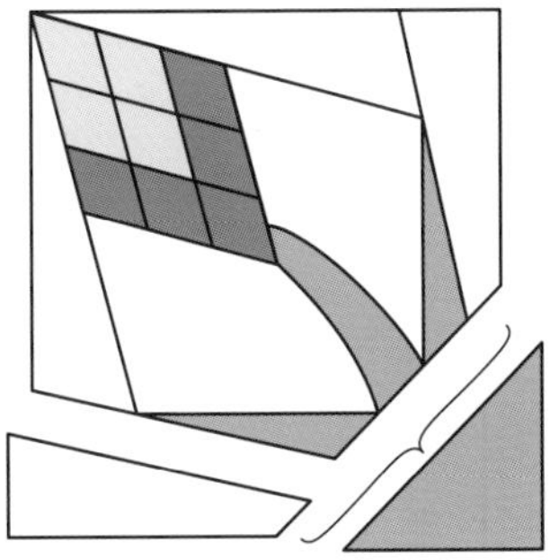

Step 5

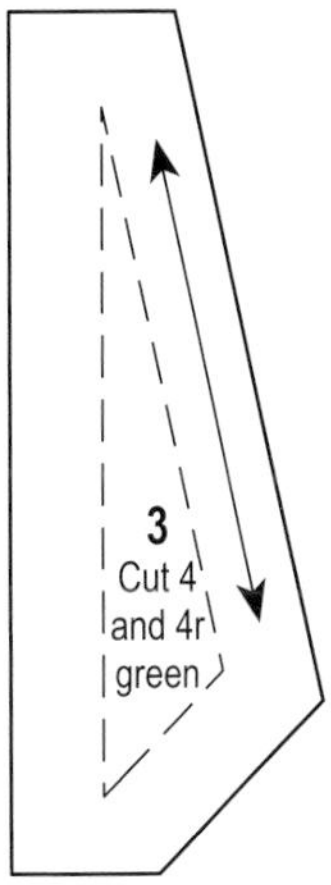

Step 6

4
Cut 4 and 4r background

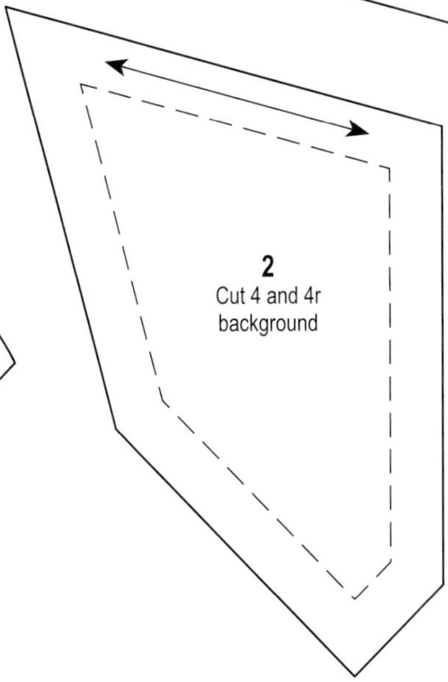

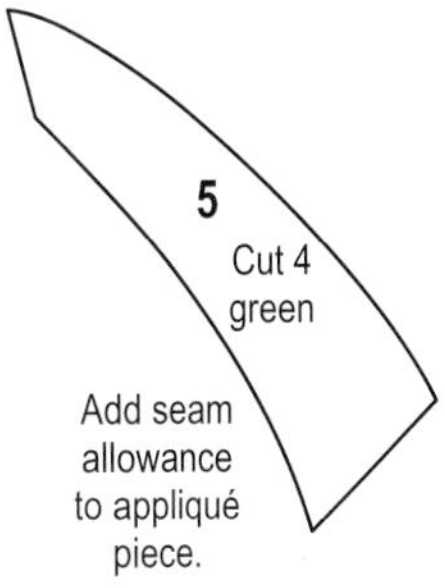

5
Cut 4 green

Add seam allowance to appliqué piece.

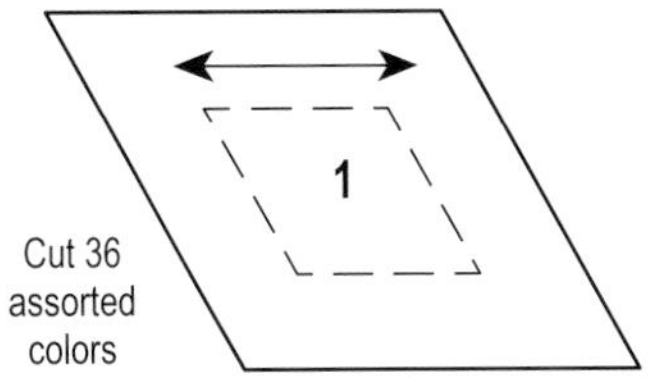

2
Cut 4 and 4r background

1
Cut 36 assorted colors

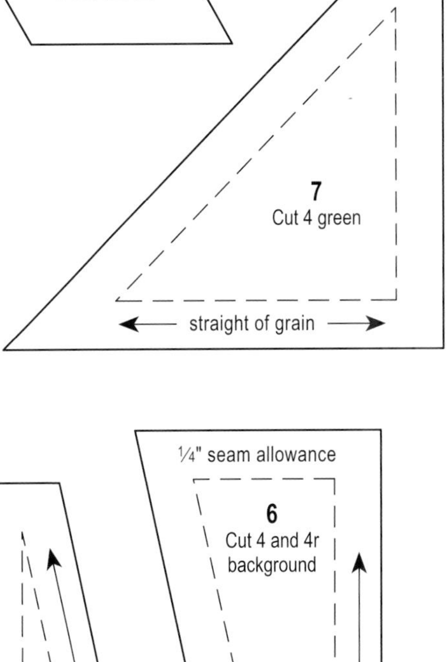

7
Cut 4 green
straight of grain

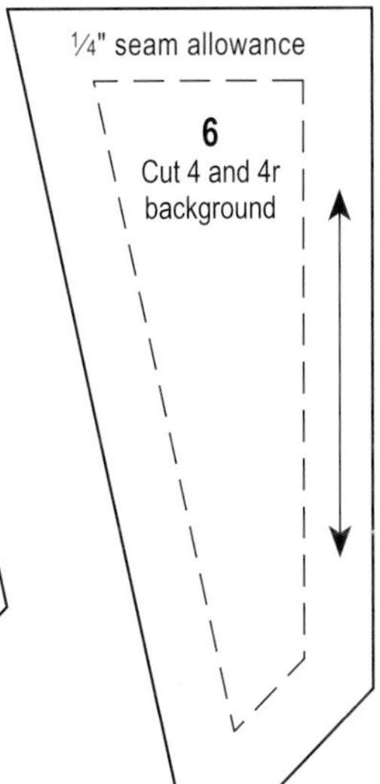

¼" seam allowance

6
Cut 4 and 4r background

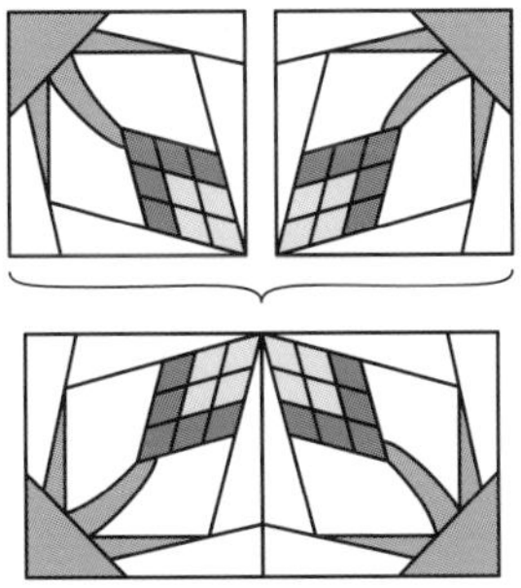

3
Cut 4 and 4r green

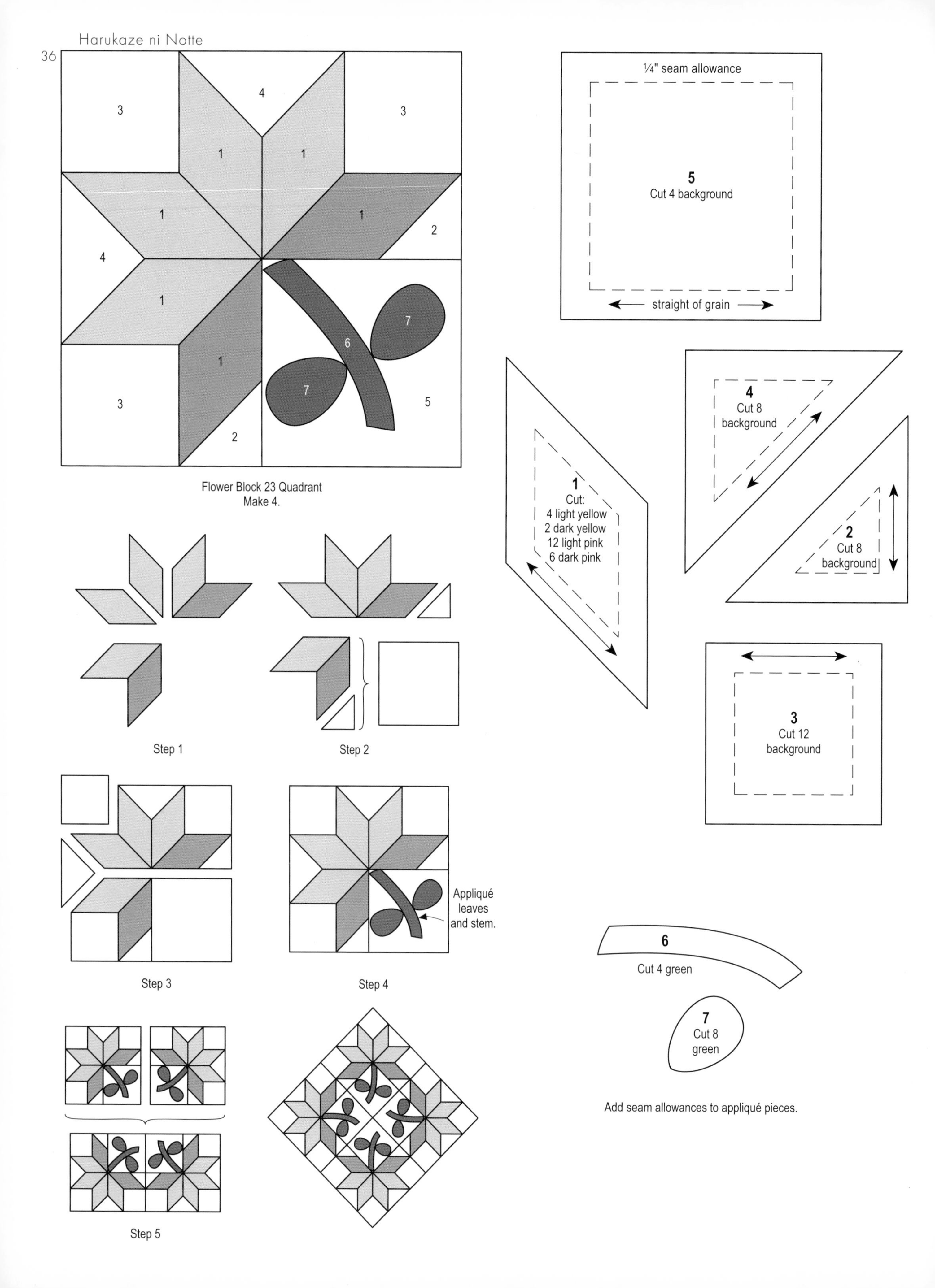
3
4
3
1
1
1
1
2
4
1
6
7
7
1
3
5
2
Flower Block 23 Quadrant
Make 4.
Step 1
Step 2
Step 3
Step 4
Appliqué
leaves
and stem.
Step 5
¼" seam allowance
5
Cut 4 background
straight of grain
1
Cut:
4 light yellow
2 dark yellow
12 light pink
6 dark pink
4
Cut 8
background
2
Cut 8
background
3
Cut 12
background
6
Cut 4 green
7
Cut 8
green
Add seam allowances to appliqué pieces.

Assemble Blocks #1, #13, and #25.

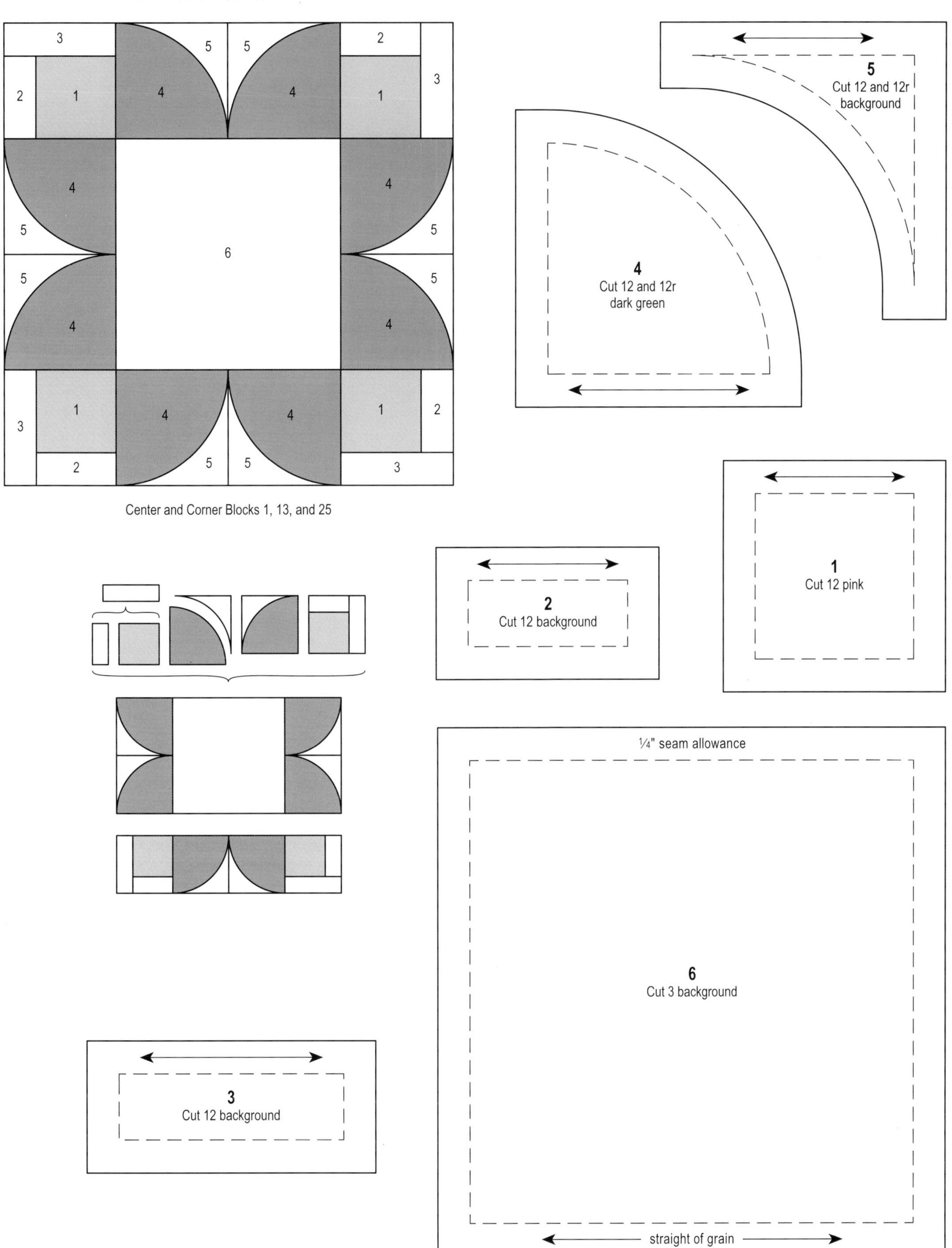

Center and Corner Blocks 1, 13, and 25

Appliqué the 3½" center squares of blocks #1 and #13, following the placement diagram and piecing order. Sign and date the center square of block #25.

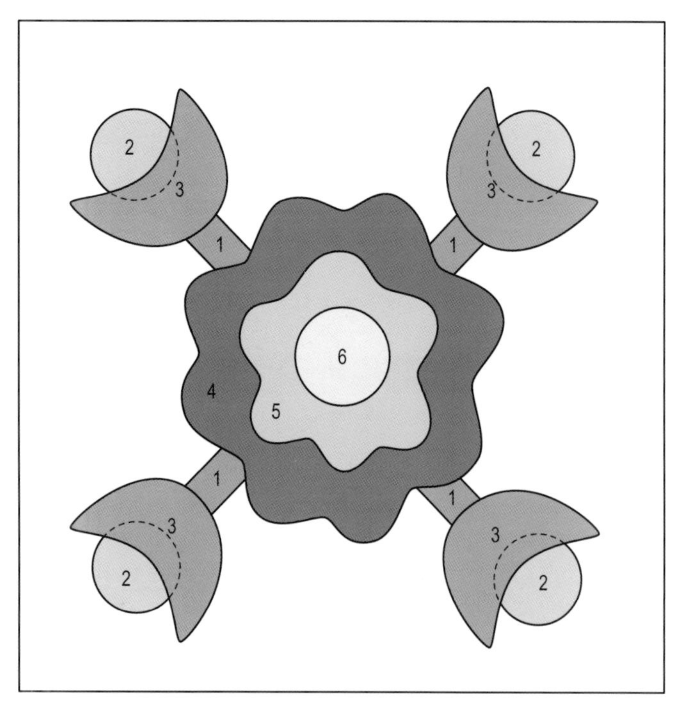

Corner Block 1
Appliqué Placement Diagram

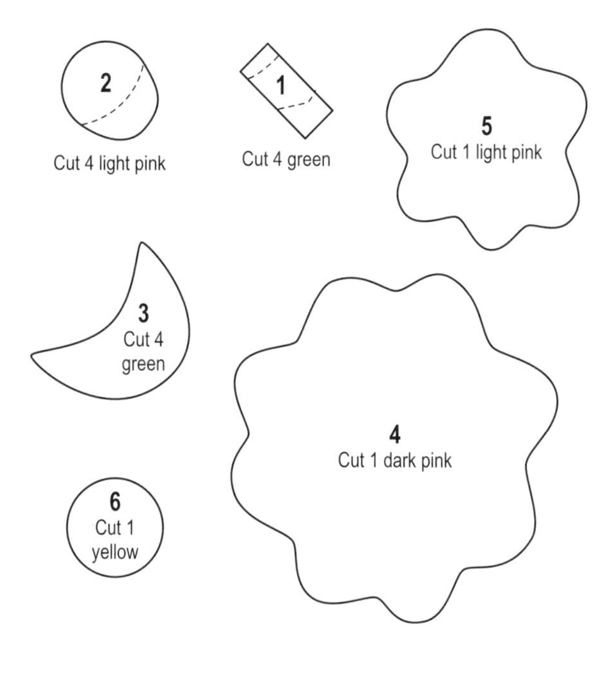

Add seam allowances to appliqué pieces.

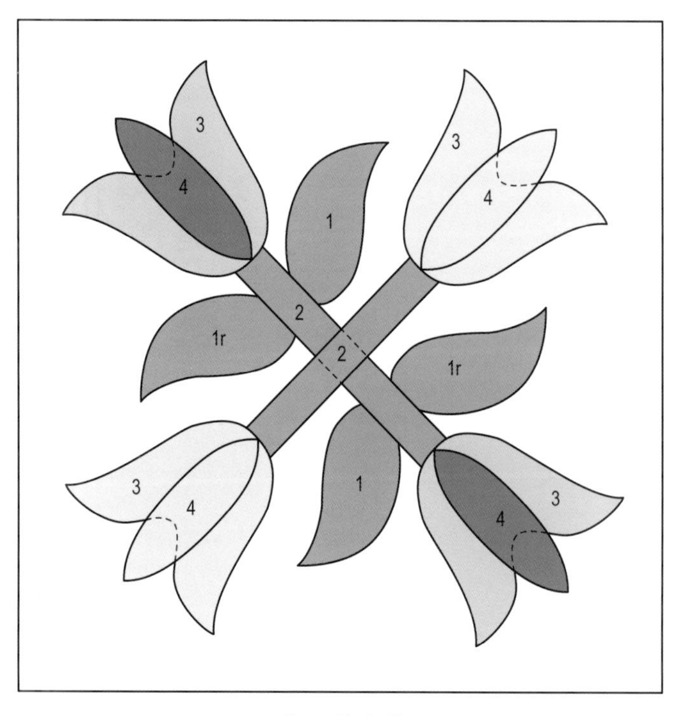

Center Block 13
Appliqué Placement Diagram

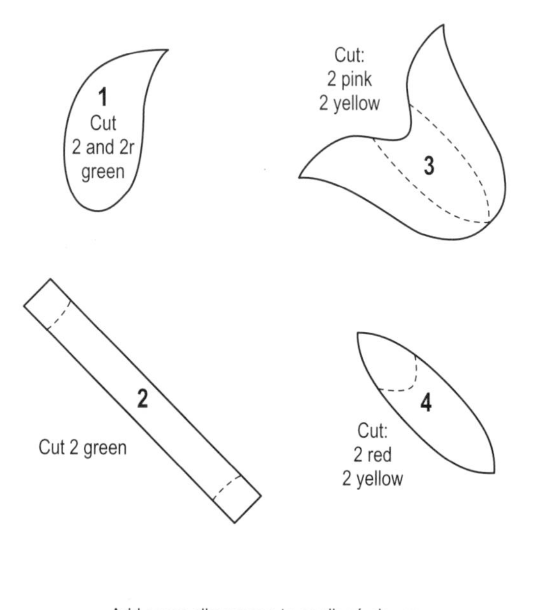

Add seam allowances to appliqué pieces.

Quilt Top Assembly

1. Along the fabric G raw edges of each of the Log Cabin background blocks, *carefully* measure 1¾" from each corner and make a mark on the *edge* of the block (*not* the seam line). Draw a line connecting the points. Trim along this line.

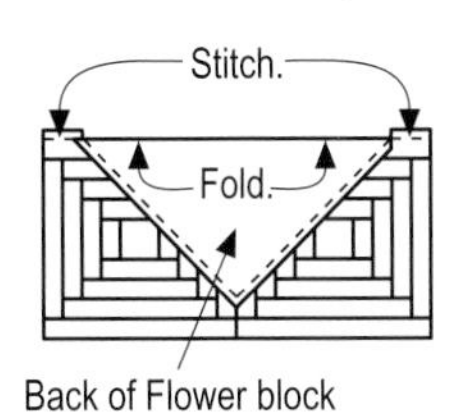

2. Sew the diagonal edge of a Log Cabin block to each side of a Flower block, starting and stopping ¼" from the edge. Press the seams toward the Flower block.

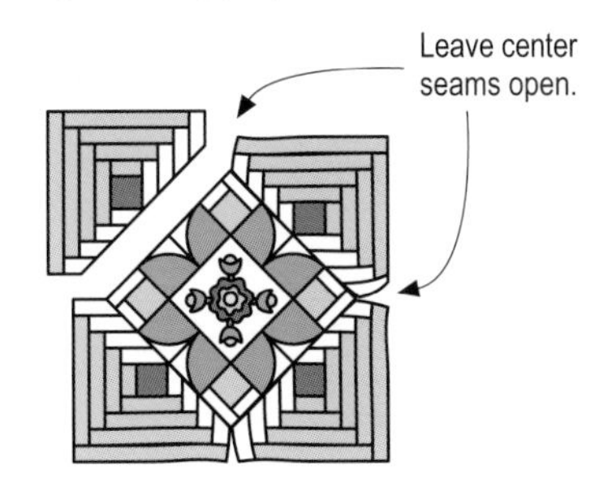

Note: Handle the Log Cabin block with care to prevent distorting the bias edges.

3. Join each of the Log Cabin blocks' center seams as you would sew mitered corners. Press the seams open.

4. Arrange Log Cabin and Flower blocks #1–#25, referring to the diagram. Sew blocks into rows, pressing the seam allowances in opposite directions from row to row. Sew the rows together.

5. Following the diagram, arrange the side blocks so the light portion of the blocks lies along the outer edges. Sew side blocks L1–5 and R1–5 into the side rows. Sew side blocks T1–5 and B1–5 into the top (T) and bottom (B) rows. Sew a corner block to each end of the top and bottom rows.
6. Sew the side rows to the sides of the quilt top, then add top and bottom rows.

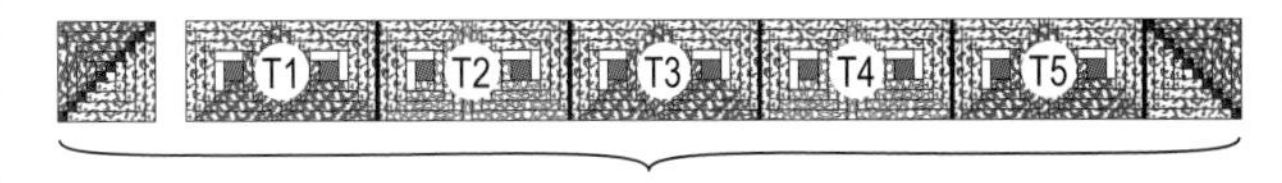

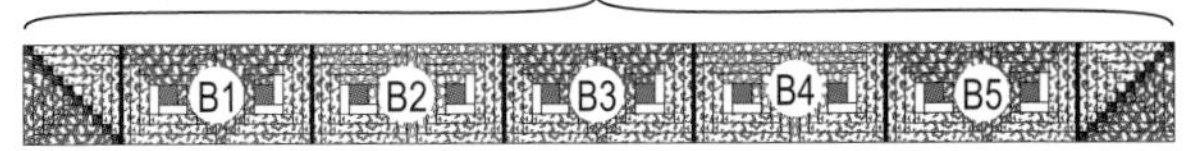

Finishing

1. Layer the quilt top with batting and backing; baste.
2. Quilt as desired. For the Flower blocks, Fujie Fukuhara outline-quilted the flower pieces. For the center Log Cabin blocks, she quilted along the center of the strips and quilted a wave design in the Log Cabin borders.
3. Bind the edges.

Kantou Matsuri ▶ *(Lantern Festival)* by *Takako Onoyama*

◀ Tangonosekku *(Boy's Day)* by *Takako Onoyama*

Tangonosekku *(Boy's Day)*

Finished quilt size: 27½" x 33" (27½" x 34½" without hanging rods)

If the Hinamatsuri *is a girl's festival, then* Sekku *celebrates boys each year on May 5. When a boy is born, people decorate the insides of their homes with miniature Japanese suits of armor and hang* koi nobori *(carp-shaped wind socks or streamers) high in the sky. In the city,* koi nobori *have become rare, but when I see these brightly colored carp "swimming" high over the roofs of apartment buildings in the refreshing May breeze, I sense the arrival of summer, and my spirit dances.*

Materials: 44"-wide fabric

1 yd. rust-blue-and-gold print for outer border
¼ yd. red-orange print for inner border
½ yd. gold-on-off-white background for fan background
½ yd. pink-and-blue sky print for fan
Assorted scraps of gold-on-black, gold-on-red, gold-on-blue, beige, black-and-white, tan, green-on-ecru, and dark brown prints for appliquéd fish
Assorted scraps of blue ombré (a print with gradated light to dark areas), light purple, blue, and green prints for mountain and clouds
6" x 6" square of white flannel for snow
1 yd. for backing
Tan embroidery floss
2 wooden dowels, each 1" x 27½"
Fabric glue or hot glue
5¾ yds. heavy black string or cording
2 goldstone, onyx, or serpentine ornaments, each 2" in diameter, with holes for hanging

Cutting

Cut all strips across the width of the fabric from selvage to selvage unless otherwise noted.

From the rust-blue-and-gold print, cut:
1 rectangle, 13" x 30"
1 rectangle, 10" x 30"
2 strips, each 4½" x 18"

From the red-orange print, cut:
2 strips, each 2½" x 22"

From the gold-on-off-white background, cut:
1 rectangle, 14" x 22"

From the pink-and-blue sky print, cut:
1 rectangle, 14" x 21"

Assembly

1. Trace the appliqué patterns, referring to the placement diagram on the pullout. Cut 1 of each fabric piece, adding a scant ¼"-wide seam allowance except for the lower "snow line" of the snow pattern. Add a seam allowance to this piece on the top and side edges only. Prepare all pieces for appliqué, using your favorite method.

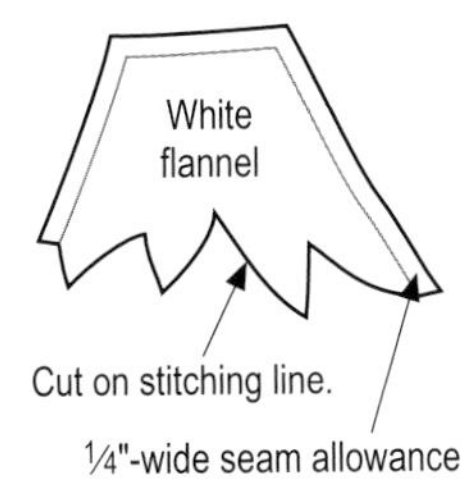

2. Transfer the fan pattern to the pink-and-blue sky fabric, but do not cut it out until the appliqué is complete.

3. Starting with the flagpole, appliqué pieces #1–#20 in numerical order. For the flannel snow (piece #16), secure the raw edge of the snow line with a running stitch.

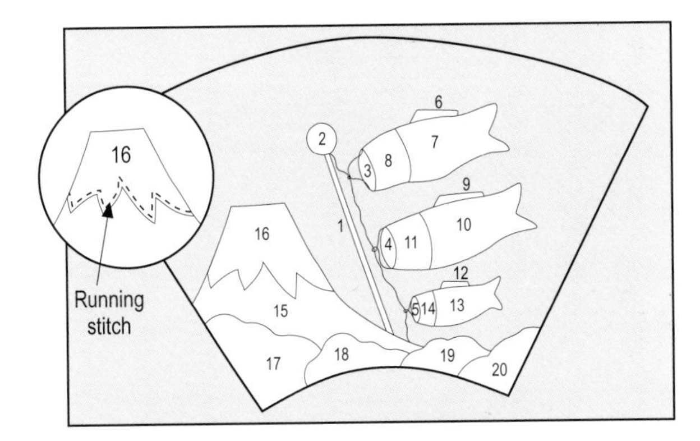

4. Couch 4 strands of embroidery floss for the rope holding the fish. To couch, bring the floss out at the top of the flagpole. With a second thread the same color as the floss, take a tiny stitch across the floss, anchoring it to the background. Run the couching thread under the background fabric and bring it through to the front about ½" from the previous stitch. Take another tiny stitch across the floss. Repeat, couching the "rope" and ending at the lower edge of Mt. Fuji. Bring the floss and couching thread to the back and tie off.

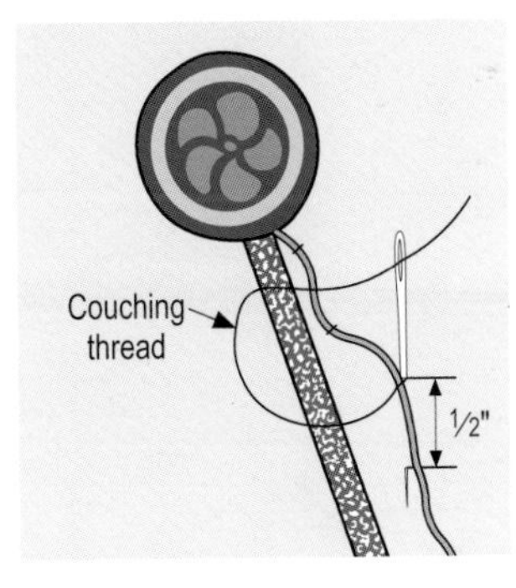

5. Bring a strand of floss out at the top of the streamer opening, loop it under the couched floss, and insert it at the bottom of the opening. With the couching thread, secure the floss, using tiny couching stitches.

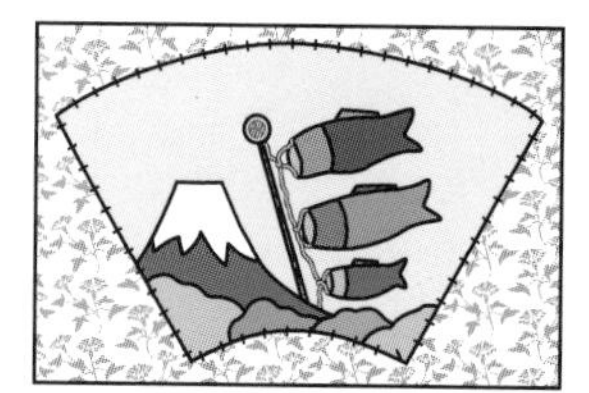

6. Cut out the fan; center and appliqué it to the 14" x 22" gold-on-off-white fabric.

Borders

1. Sew a 2½" x 22" red-orange print strip to the top and bottom edges of the quilt top. Sew a 4½" x 18" rust-blue-and-gold print strip to each side of the quilt top.

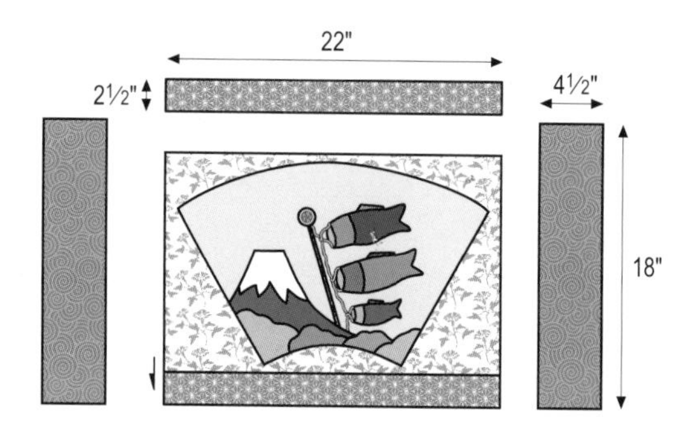

2. Sew the 13" x 30" rust-blue-and-gold print rectangle to the top edge of the quilt, and the 10" x 30" rectangle to the bottom edge of the quilt. Press the seam allowances toward the strips.

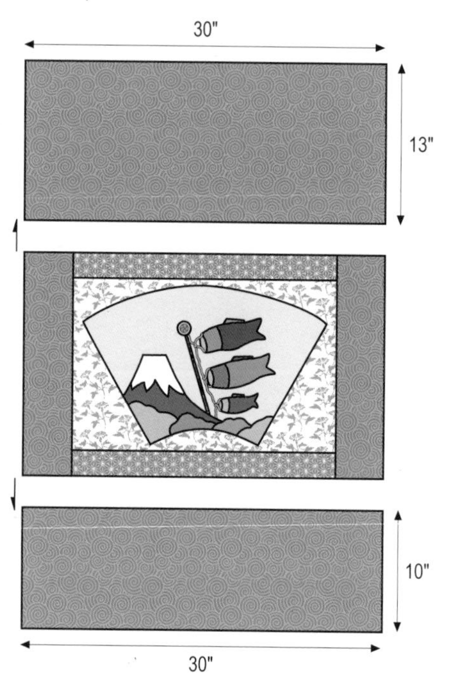

Finishing

1. Layer the quilt top with batting and backing; baste.
2. Quilt around the appliqué shapes; quilt the sky, clouds, and borders as desired.
3. Trim the batting and backing to measure 27½" x 40". Trim the quilt top to extend 1¼" beyond the batting and backing.

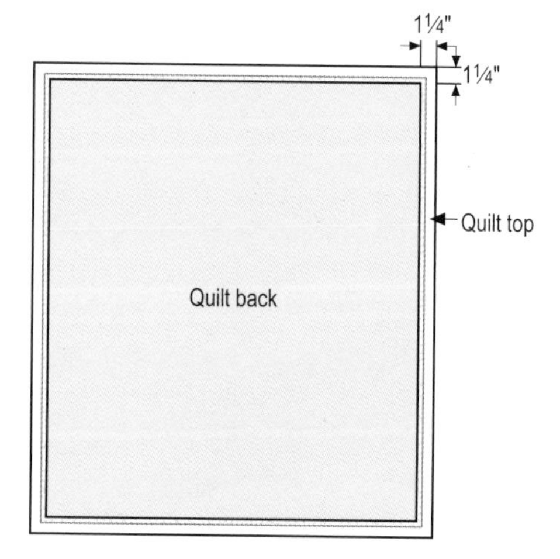

4. Turn under ¼" along the top and bottom edges of the quilt top, then fold the fabric to the back of the quilt to create a 1"-wide binding. Hand stitch the binding to the back of the quilt. Repeat with the side edges.

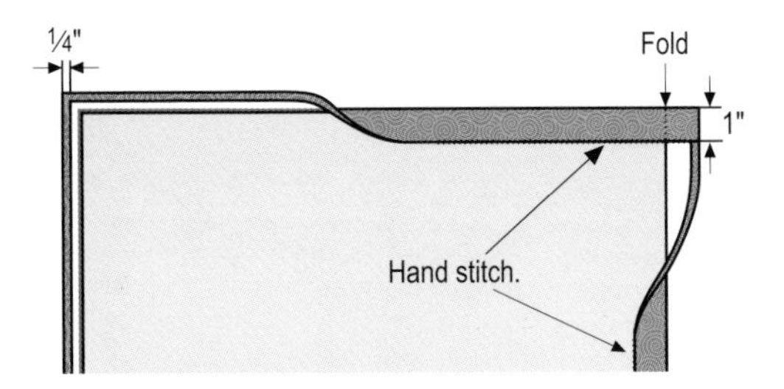

5. Fold 2½" of the top and bottom edges of the quilt top to the back to make the rod pockets. Hand stitch in place.

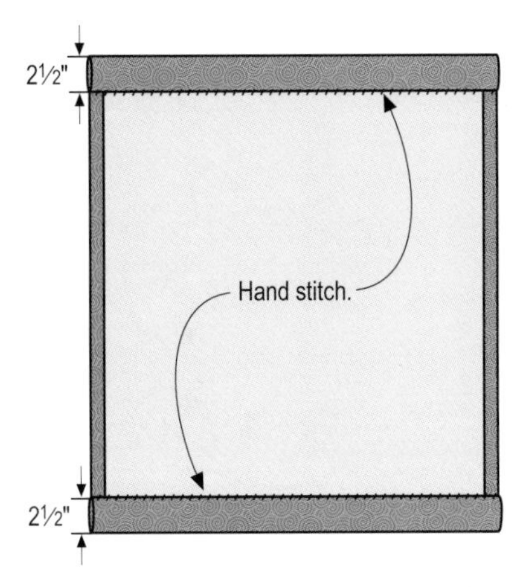

6. Using fabric or hot glue, glue scraps of the rust-blue-and-gold print over the ends of the dowels. When the glue is dry, insert the dowels into the pockets and hand stitch the pocket to the dowel cover. Stitch the pocket opening to secure the dowel in the pocket.

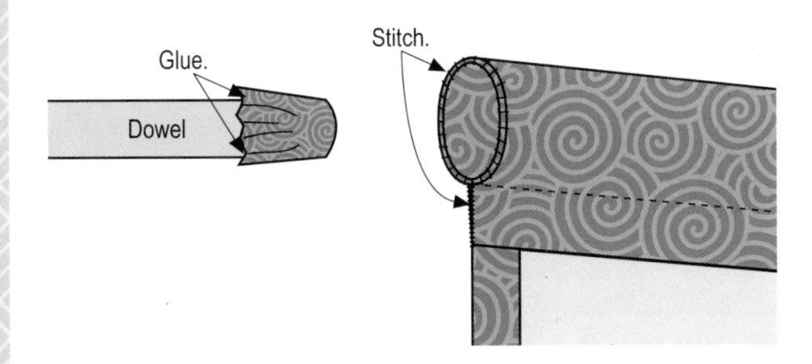

7. Cut 4 strands of black string or cording, each 20" long. Fold each pair of cords in half and insert the loop through the hole in each of the ornaments. Bring the cord ends through the loop as shown.

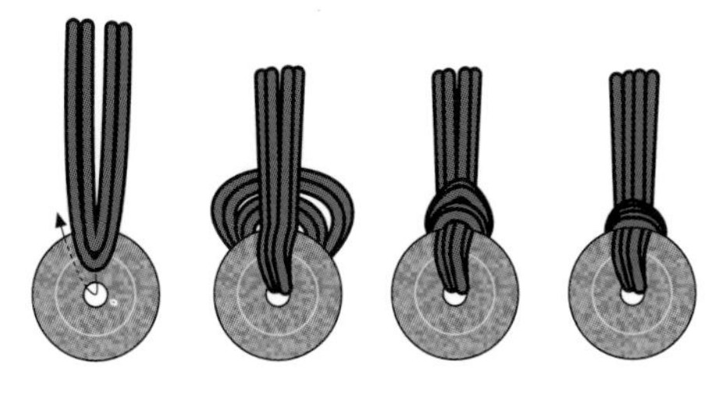

8. Center the ornaments on the front of the quilt and stitch the cord ends securely to the back and top of the top rod pocket.

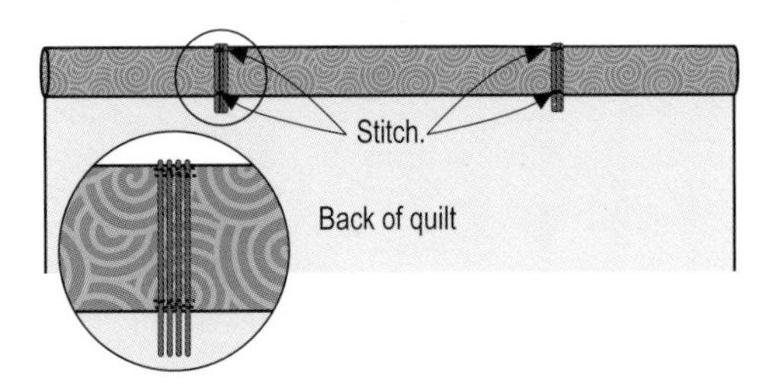

9. Cut 3 more strands of cording, each 40" long. Treating the 3 strands as 1, tie a knot at each end, leaving 2"-long tails. Securely stitch each knot to the fabric covering the ends of the dowel.

Note: The photo on page 40 shows the hanging cords secured to the center of the quilt. The cords pulled the fabric, so after the photo, I resewed the cord ends to the ends of the dowel.

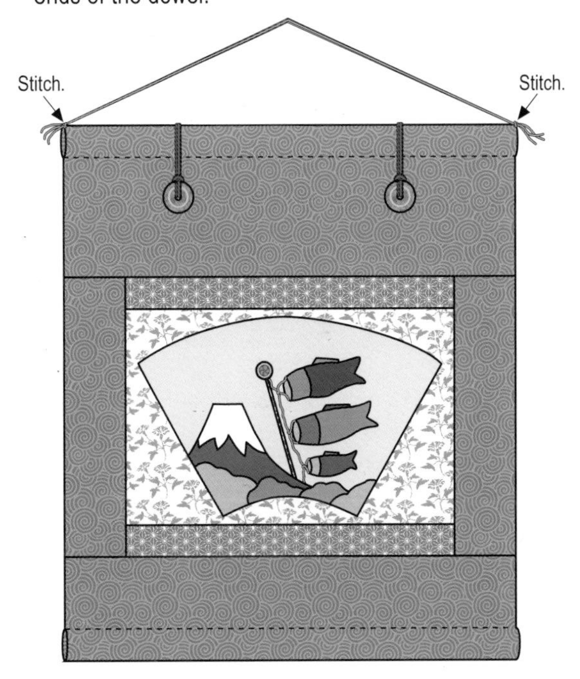

Kantou Matsuri *(Lantern Festival)*

Finished quilt size: 52½" x 41½"
Finished block size: 7½" x 7½"

Every year from August 5–7, Akita prefecture holds its annual Bamboo Lantern Festival. Young men balance long bamboo poles on their shoulders and foreheads. Forty-six brightly colored paper lanterns hang from several horizontal poles attached to the top of each bamboo pole. The young men, clad in traditional festive garb, perform with these enormous luminous structures in a style unchanged since the beginning of the Edo period, about four hundred years ago.

I am especially moved by this festival, since it is held at the birthplace of my mother, who passed away at an early age.

This wall hanging was inspired by the design of the young men's Happi *coats, coupled with the image of the lanterns.*

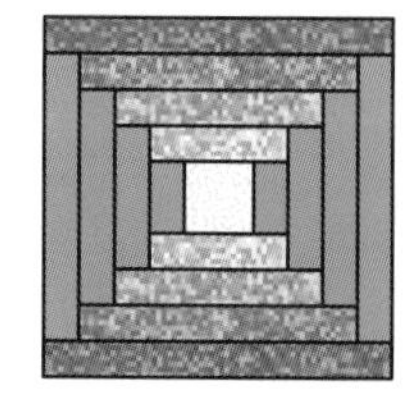

Block A

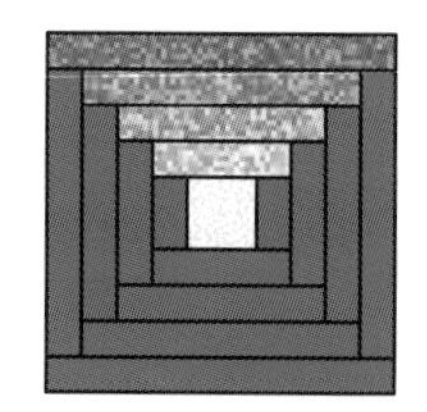

Block B

Materials: 44"-wide fabric

1½ yds. *total* of 7 assorted yellow, yellow-orange, and orange prints for Log Cabin blocks
¾ yd. *total* of 5 assorted blue prints for Log Cabin blocks
1¼ yds. *total* of 4 assorted black prints for Log Cabin blocks and narrow binding
⅓ yd. black-and-white print for collar, and for cuff and skirt binding
1⅝ yds. for backing
50" x 60" piece of batting

Cutting

Cut all strips across the width of the fabric from selvage to selvage unless otherwise noted.

From one of the yellow-orange prints, cut:
2 strips, each 2" wide; then cut 30 squares, each 2" x 2", for segment #1.

From the remaining 6 yellow, yellow-orange, and orange prints, cut 30 strips, each 1¼" wide; then cut rectangles in the following sizes:
46 rectangles, each 1¼" x 3½", for segment #3
46 rectangles, each 1¼" x 5", for segment #5
46 rectangles, each 1¼" x 6½", for segment #7
46 rectangles, each 1¼" x 8", for segment #9

From the assorted blue prints, cut 17 strips, each 1¼" wide; then cut rectangles in the following sizes:
32 rectangles, each 1¼" x 2", for segment #2
32 rectangles, each 1¼" x 3½", for segment #4
32 rectangles, each 1¼" x 5", for segment #6
32 rectangles, each 1¼" x 6½", for segment #8

From the darkest black print, cut:
4 strips, each 1" wide, for binding

From the remaining black prints, cut 21 strips, each 1½" wide; then cut the following number of rectangles:
28 rectangles, each 1¼" x 2", for segment #2
42 rectangles, each 1¼" x 3½", for segments #3 and #4
42 rectangles, each 1¼" x 5", for segments #5 and #6
42 rectangles, each 1¼" x 6½", for segments #7 and #8
14 rectangles, each 1¼" x 8", for segment #9

From the black-and-white print, cut:
2 strips, each 2½" x 23", for cuff binding
1 rectangle, 4½" x 23", for skirt binding
1 rectangle, 4½" x 10½", for collar

From the backing fabric, cut:
2 strips, each 5" wide

Block Assembly

Block A

1. Sew a blue segment #2 to opposite sides of a yellow-orange segment #1. Press seam allowances toward segment #2.

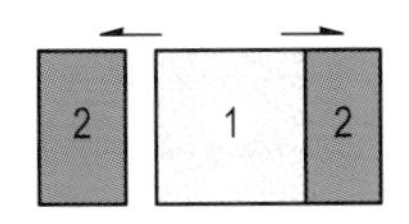

2. Sew a yellow-orange segment #3 to opposite sides of the unit made in step 1; then sew a blue segment #4 to the other 2 sides of the unit as shown. Press all seam allowances toward the outer edges of the block.

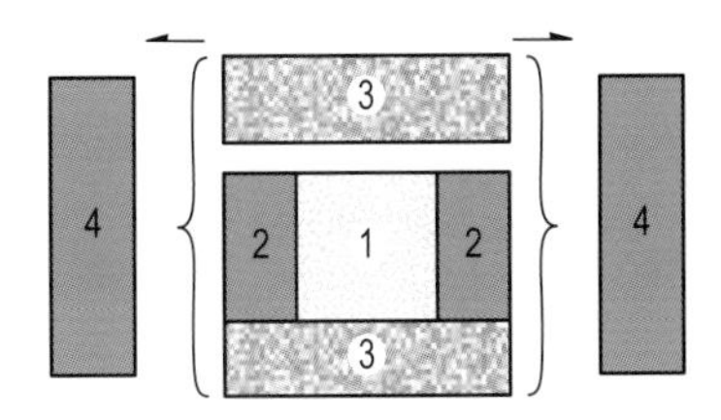

3. Continue sewing segments #5–#9 to opposite sides of the unit, alternating orange and blue segments in numerical order.

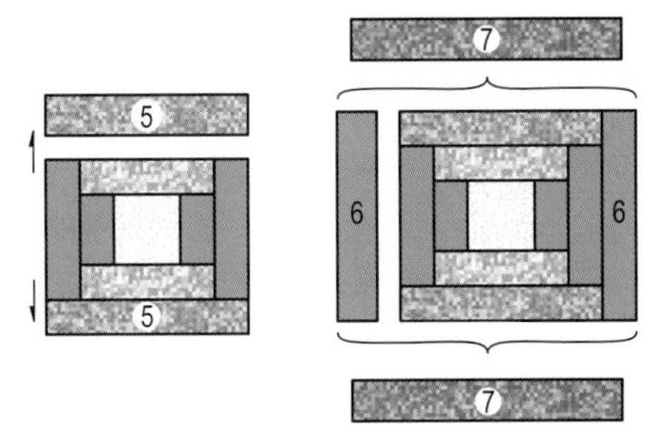

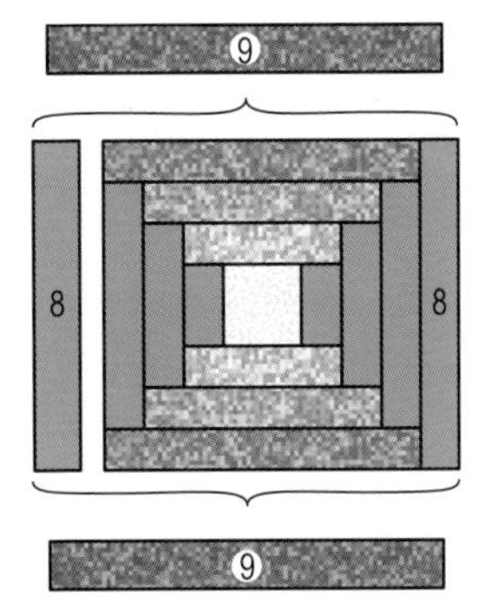

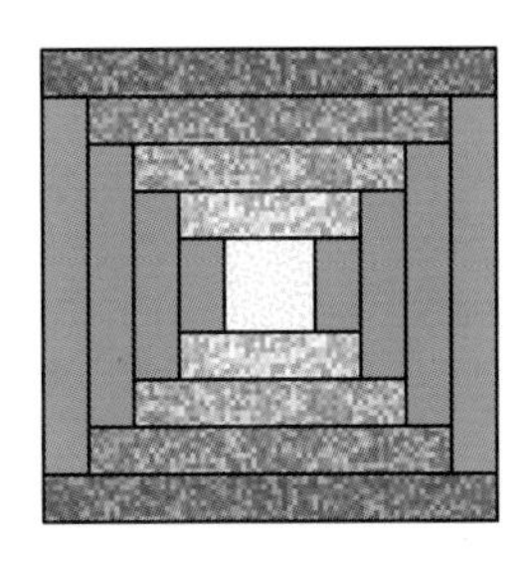

Block A
Make 16.

Block B

1. Sew a black segment #2 to opposite sides of a yellow-orange segment #1. Press seam allowances toward segment #2.

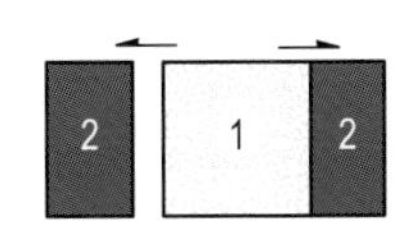

2. Sew a yellow-orange segment #3 to one side of the unit made in step 1, and a black segment #3 to the opposite side. Sew a black segment #4 to the other 2 sides of the unit as shown. Press all seam allowances toward the outer edges of the block.

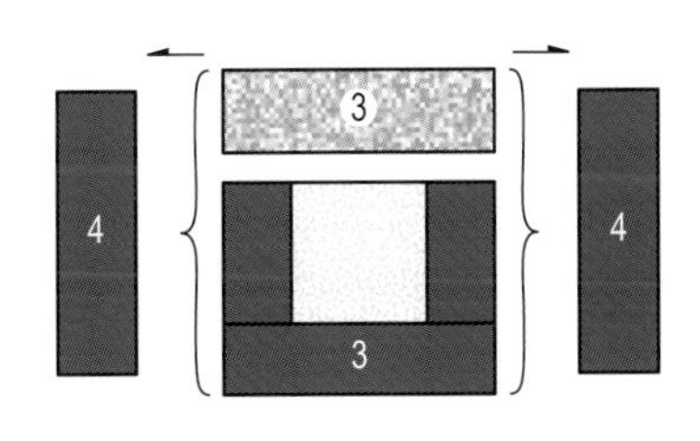

3. Continue sewing segments #5–#9 to opposite sides of the unit, following the diagram for color placement.

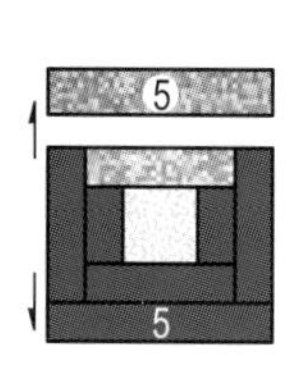

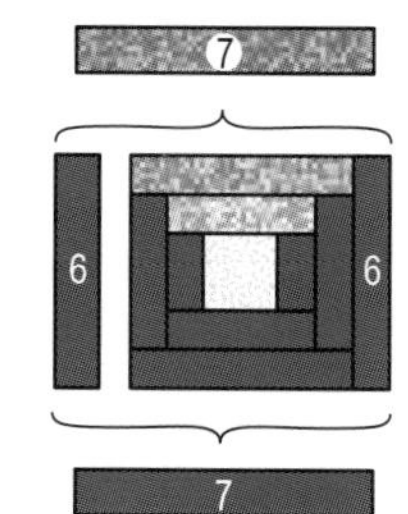

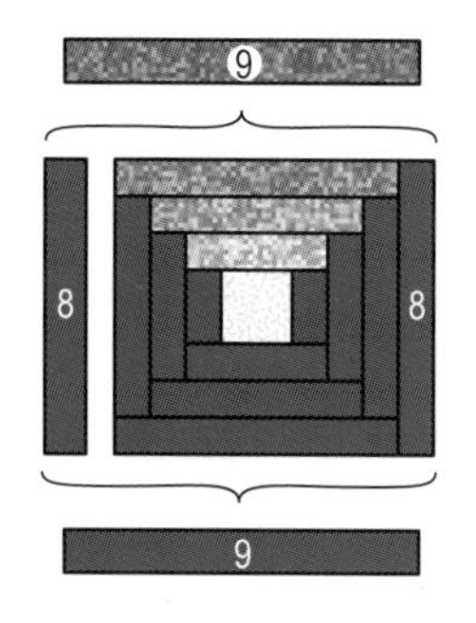

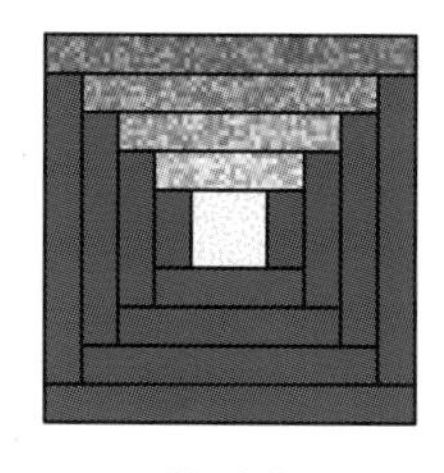

Block B
Make 14.

Quilt Top Assembly

1. Arrange the blocks, referring to the diagram for color and block placement. Sew the blocks into rows, pressing the seam allowances as shown. Sew the rows together.

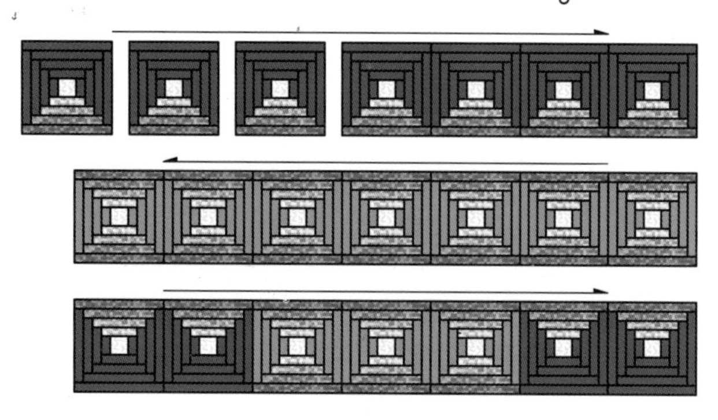

2. Cut an 18" x 25" rectangle from a corner of the backing fabric as shown. Sew the rectangle to the remaining backing to form a *kimono* shape.

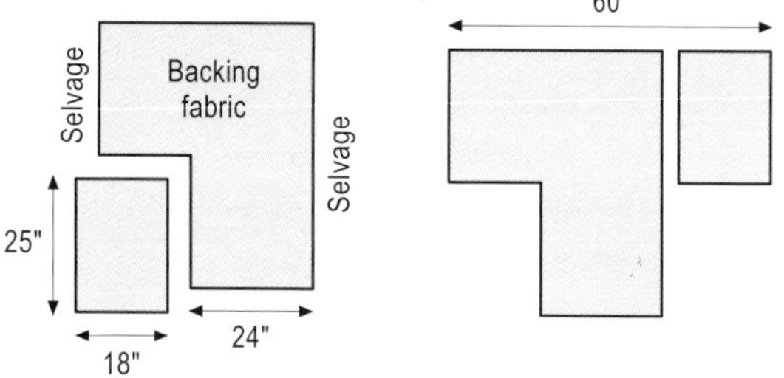

Finishing

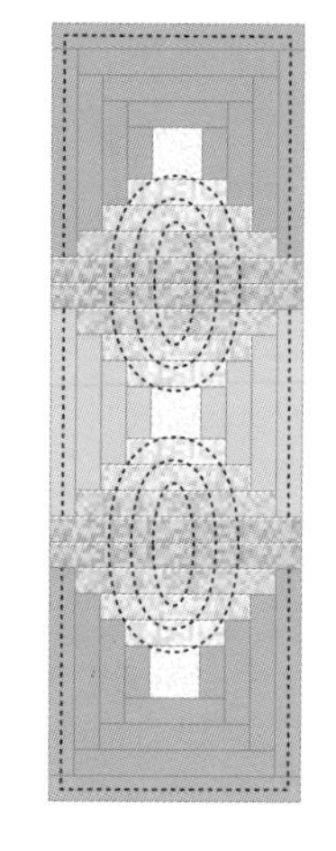

1. Layer the quilt top with batting and backing; baste.
2. Quilt as desired. I chose straight lines for dark areas, and ovals in the light areas to represent the lanterns.
3. Trim the batting and backing even with the edges of the quilt top, except leave about 2" of batting extending beyond the lower edge and sleeve ends.
4. Join the 1"-wide black print binding strips end to end. Sew the binding to the edges of the quilt across the top, under the sleeves, and along the lower sides. Fold the binding to the back of the quilt, turn the raw edge under ¼", and hand stitch to the quilt.

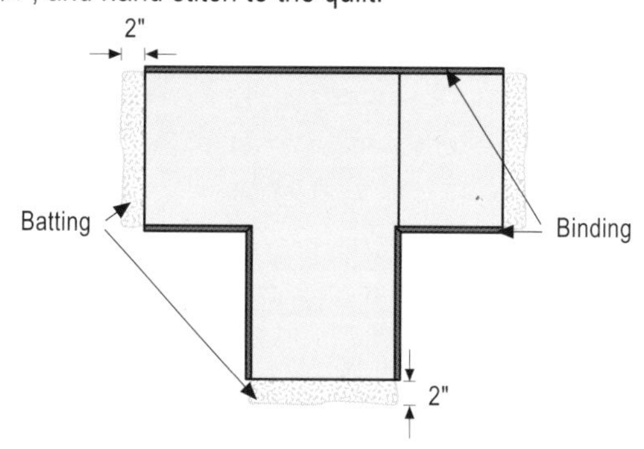

5. Sew the 2½"-wide black-and-white cuff binding to the end of one sleeve. Turn the raw edge under ¼". Press the binding toward the sleeve end. Fold the binding in half lengthwise, right sides together, and stitch across the short ends, even with the bound edge of the quilt. Trim the seam allowances to ¼". Fold the binding to the back, tucking the batting inside for extra fullness. Hand stitch to the back of the quilt. Repeat for the second sleeve.

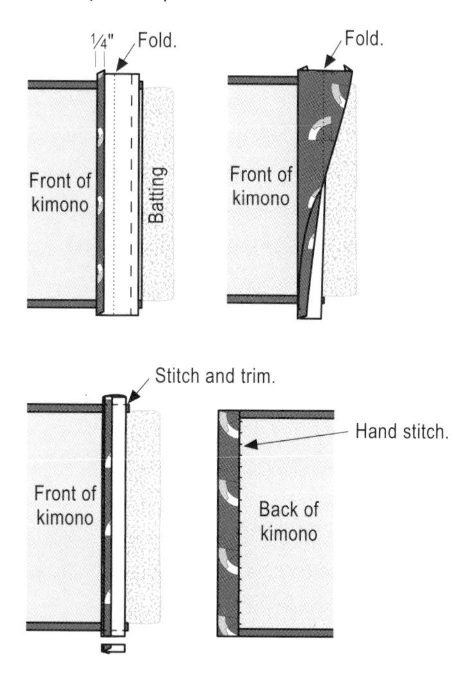

6. Sew the black-and-white skirt binding to the lower edge, following the instructions given in step 5 for the cuff binding.

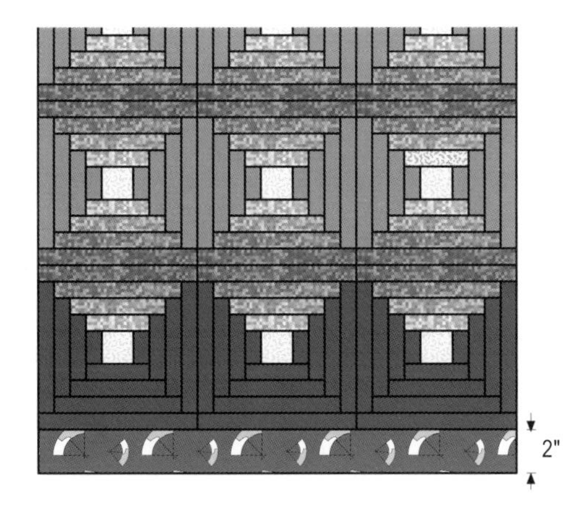

7. Fold the 4½" x 10½" black-and-white rectangle in half lengthwise, right sides together. Layer a 2¼" x 10½" piece of batting over the folded rectangle. Stitch each end of the rectangle at a 45° angle; trim seam allowances to ¼". Turn the collar right side out. Quilt as desired.

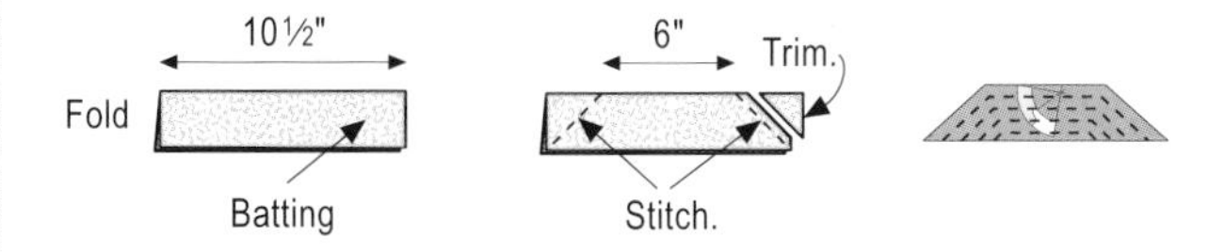

8. Place the collar in the center of the back of the quilt, with the centers matching and the raw edges of the collar extending ½" below the folded edge of the binding; baste.

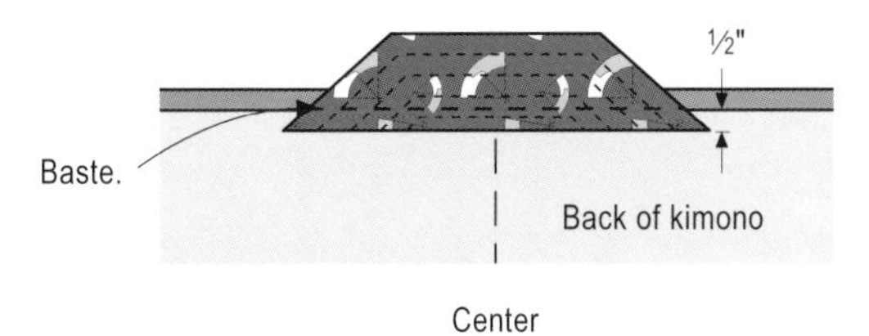

9. To make the hanging sleeve, join the 5"-wide backing strips end to end. Fold the strip in half lengthwise, wrong sides together. Stitch the raw edges together with a ¼"-wide seam allowance. Lay the sleeve flat, with the fold at the top, and press.

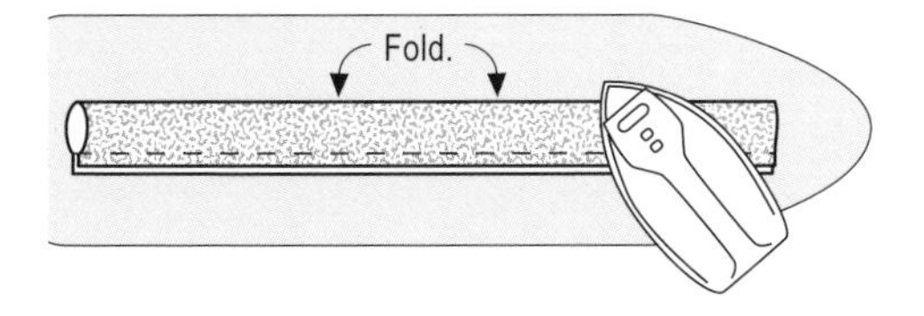

10. Measure across the width of the *kimono* from sleeve end to sleeve end. Cut the hanging sleeve to this length. Turn under ½" at each end. Pin the hanging sleeve's fold to the back of the *kimono* at the stitched edge of the binding. Turn under the lower edge of the sleeve along the stitching line; hand stitch the top and bottom edges to the *kimono*, attaching the collar at the same time.

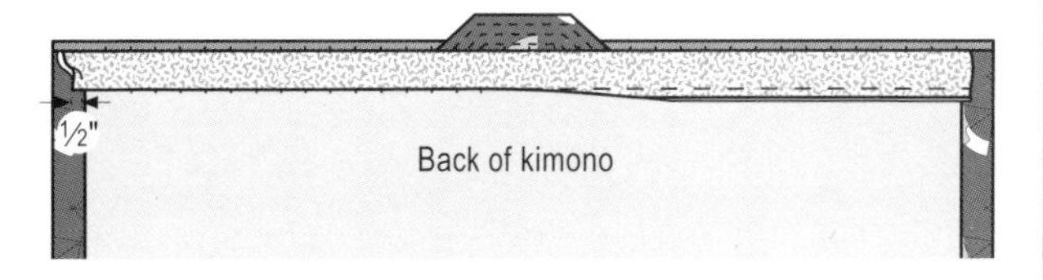

11. On the front of the *kimono*, hand stitch the edge of the binding to the collar.

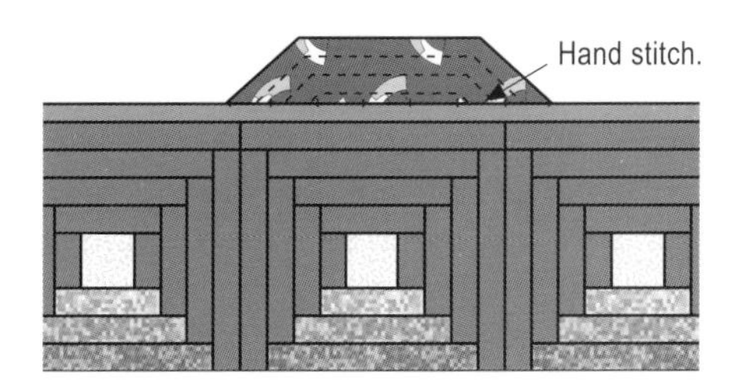

◀ Momijigari *(Tessellated Autumn Leaves) by Takako Onoyama*

Take no Haru ▶ *(Bamboo Spring) by Kumiko Maeda*

▼ Akinoyonaga *(Long Autumn Nights) by Mariko Miwa*

Momijigari *(Tessellated Autumn Leaves)*

Finished quilt size: 54" x 64"

Finished block size: 10¼" x 10¼"

As it is a tradition in Japan to view the cherry blossoms in spring, it is a tradition to enjoy the changing leaves in autumn. Inspired by the beautiful scenery, people often travel to the fields and mountains, write poetry, and make toasts with sake (Japanese rice wine, pronounced ***sah****-kay).*

Since the Heian period (794–1185 A.D.), people have gone in pursuit of scenes blazing with color and have reluctantly watched the remnants of autumn depart. Today, it is popular to go on picnics and vacations at this time of year. Recreational areas become crowded. For me, when harvest time comes around and good food and fair weather are plentiful, it is the most beautiful time of year in mainland Japan.

Materials: 44"-wide fabric

3 yds. green print for background, borders #1 and #3, and binding
20 fat eighths (9" x 22" or 11" x 18") assorted beige, orange, and rust prints for blocks
½ yd. variegated orange-rust-and-brown print for border #2
3½ yds. for backing
62" x 72" piece of batting

Cutting

Cut all strips across the width of the fabric from selvage to selvage unless otherwise noted.

From the green print, cut:
2 strips, each 2½" x 45" from the lengthwise grain, for top and bottom border #1
2 strips, each 2½" x 55" from the lengthwise grain, for side border #1
2 strips, each 4½" x 55" from the lengthwise grain, for top and bottom border #3
2 strips, each 4½" x 65" from the lengthwise grain, for side border #3
6 strips, each 1" wide, for binding
40 each of triangle B and B reversed for blocks

From each of the assorted beige, orange, and rust prints, cut:
2 triangle A, for a total of 40 triangles

From the variegated orange-rust-and-brown print, cut:
8 strips, each 1½" wide, for border #2

Assembly

1. Pin, then sew a green print triangle B and a B reversed to each short side of triangle A. Press the seam allowances toward the green triangles.

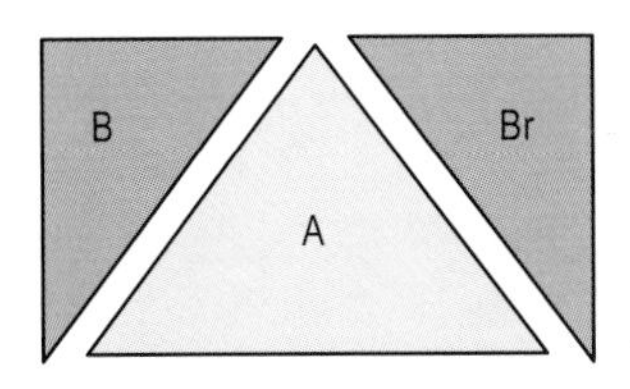

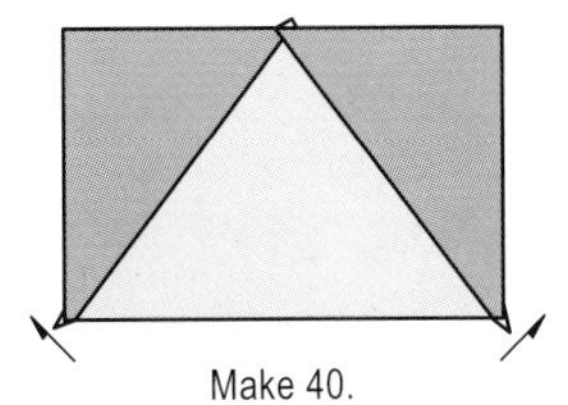

Make 40.

2. Beginning at the long unsewn edge of triangle A, cut across the unit to make 4 pieced strips, each 1¾" wide.

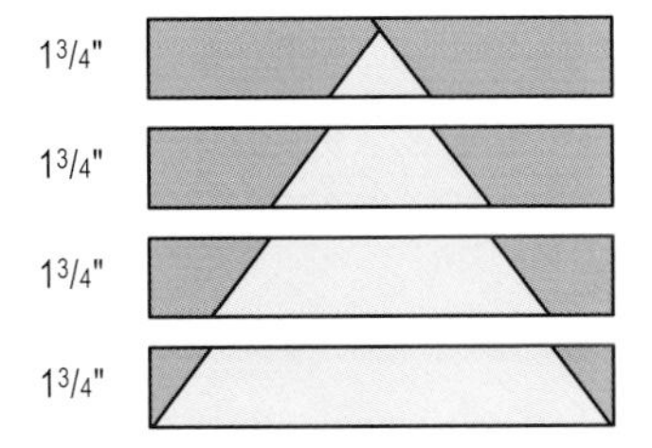

3. Without changing the order of the strips, rotate each piece 180°, then sew the strips together to make a half block. Make 20 matching pairs of half blocks.

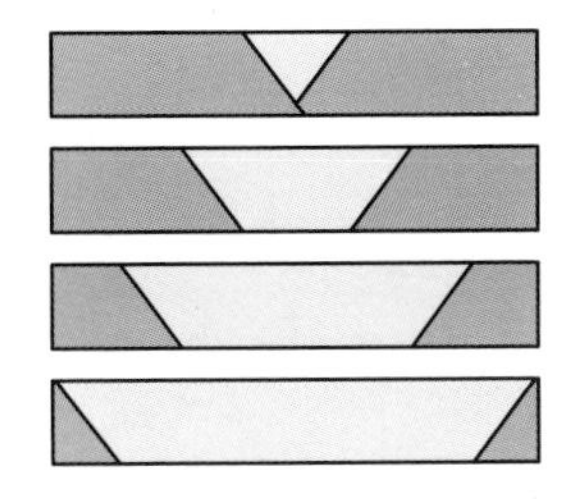

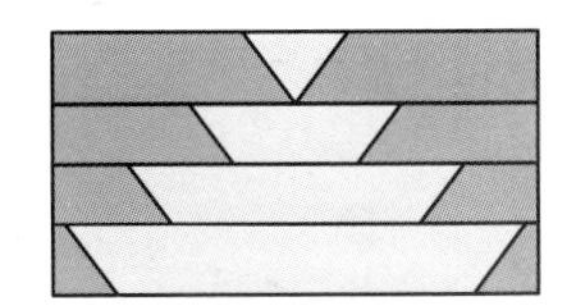

Make 20 matching pairs.

4. Join matching half blocks to make a total of 20 blocks.

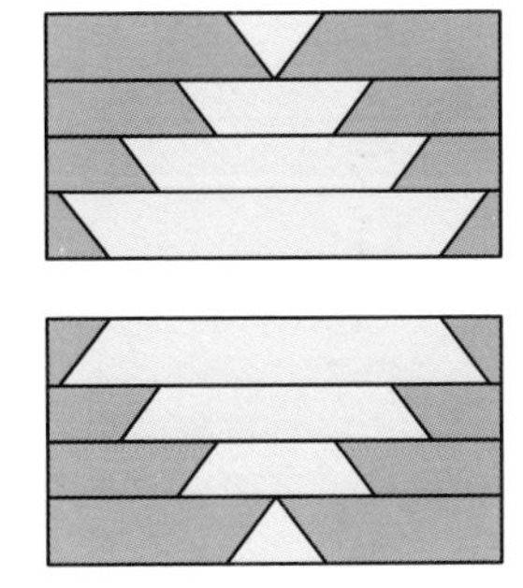

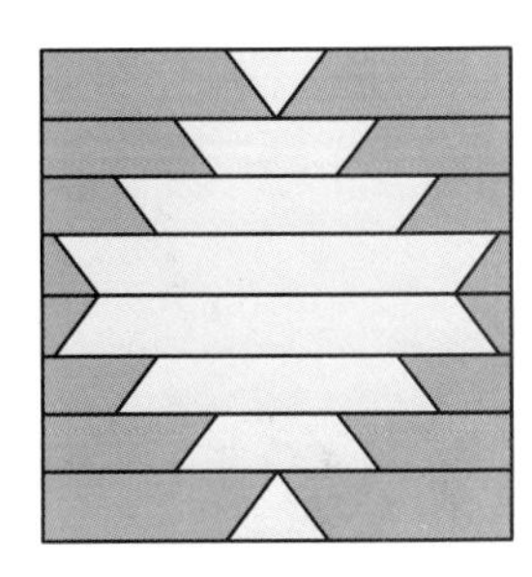

Make 20.

5. Arrange the blocks in rows, with the lightest-value blocks at the top of the quilt and the darkest-value blocks at the bottom. Sew the blocks into rows, pressing the seam allowances in opposite directions from row to row. Sew the rows together.

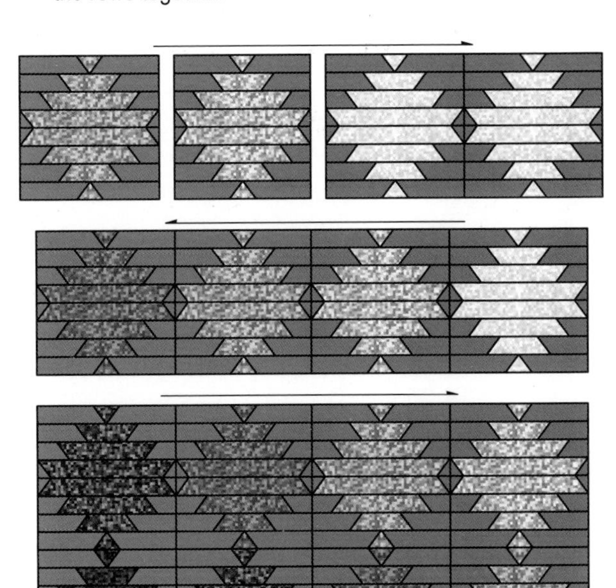

Borders

1. Sew the 1½"-wide variegated orange-rust-and-brown print strips together in pairs, end to end, to make the border #2 strips.
2. Matching the center points of each side border #1, #2, and #3, sew the strips together to make 2 pieced side borders. Repeat to make the pieced top and bottom borders. Press the seam allowances toward border #3.

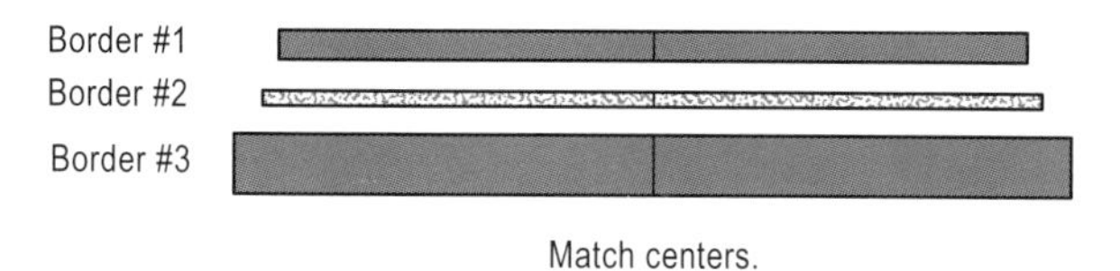

Match centers.

Make 2 side borders.
Make 2 top and bottom borders.

3. Referring to steps 6–8 of "Borders" for "Bingatazome" on page 17, stitch the borders to the quilt top.

4. Carefully align the pieced border, right sides together, matching the seam lines at the corners. Miter the corners. Trim the seam allowances to ¼", then press them open.

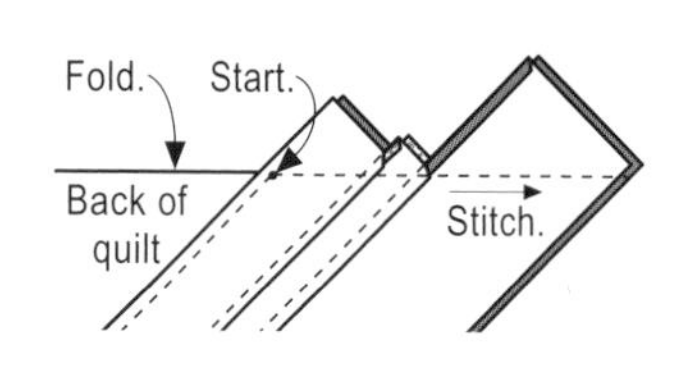

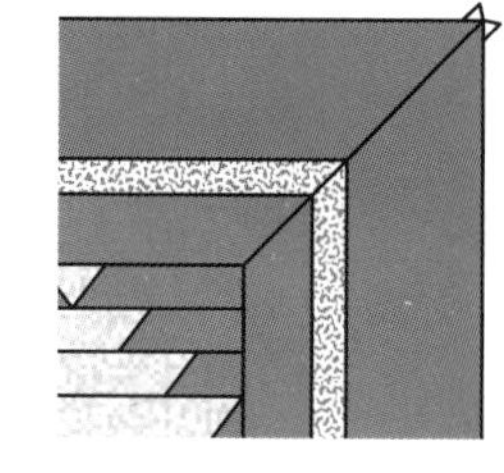

Finishing

1. Layer the quilt top with batting and backing; baste.
2. Quilt as desired. My image for this quilt design was autumn leaves falling in a stream, but feel free to use your imagination for your own design. For border #3, I used the leaf patterns on pages 56–57.
3. Bind the edges.

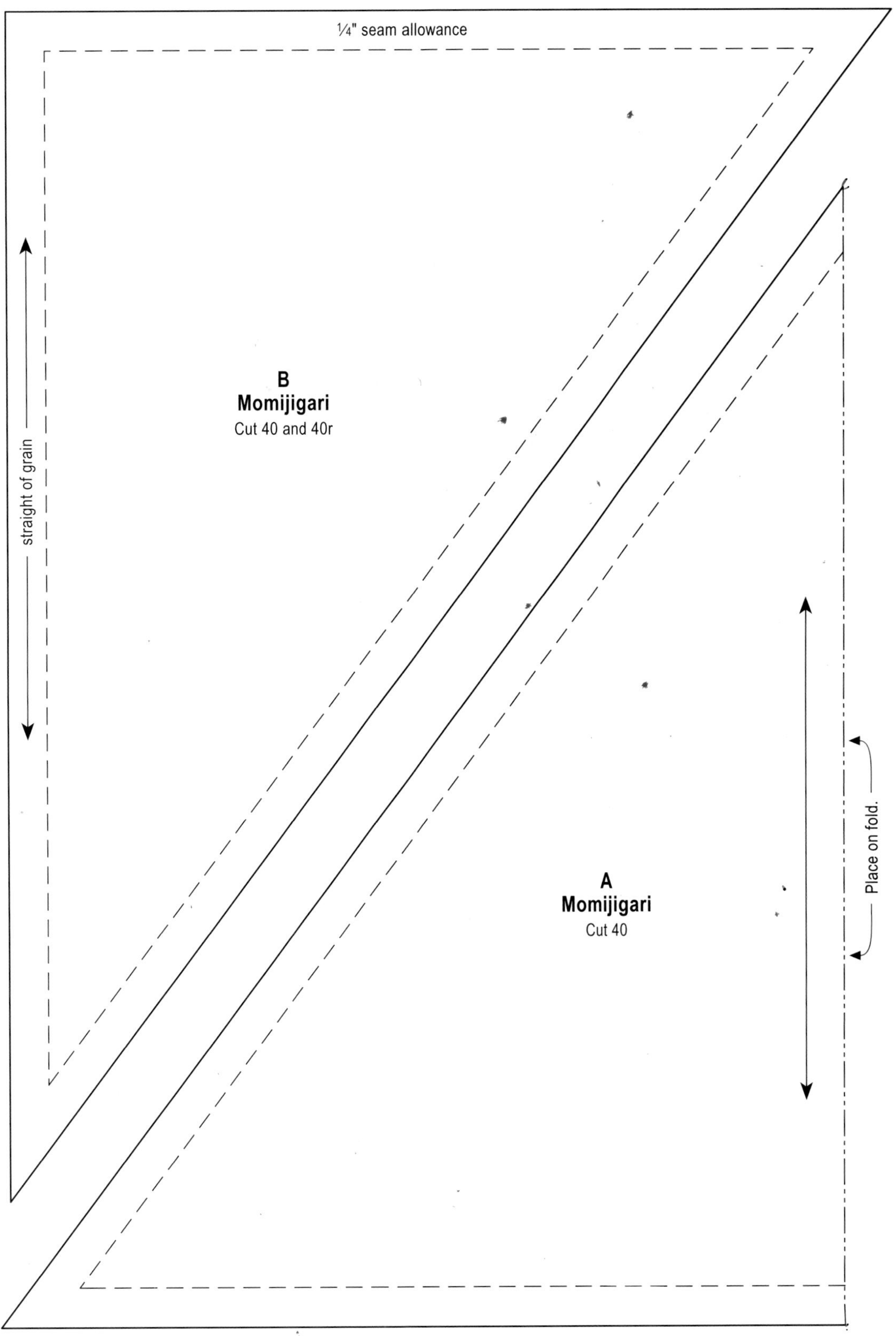
¼" seam allowance
straight of grain
B
Momijigari
Cut 40 and 40r
A
Momijigari
Cut 40
Place on fold.

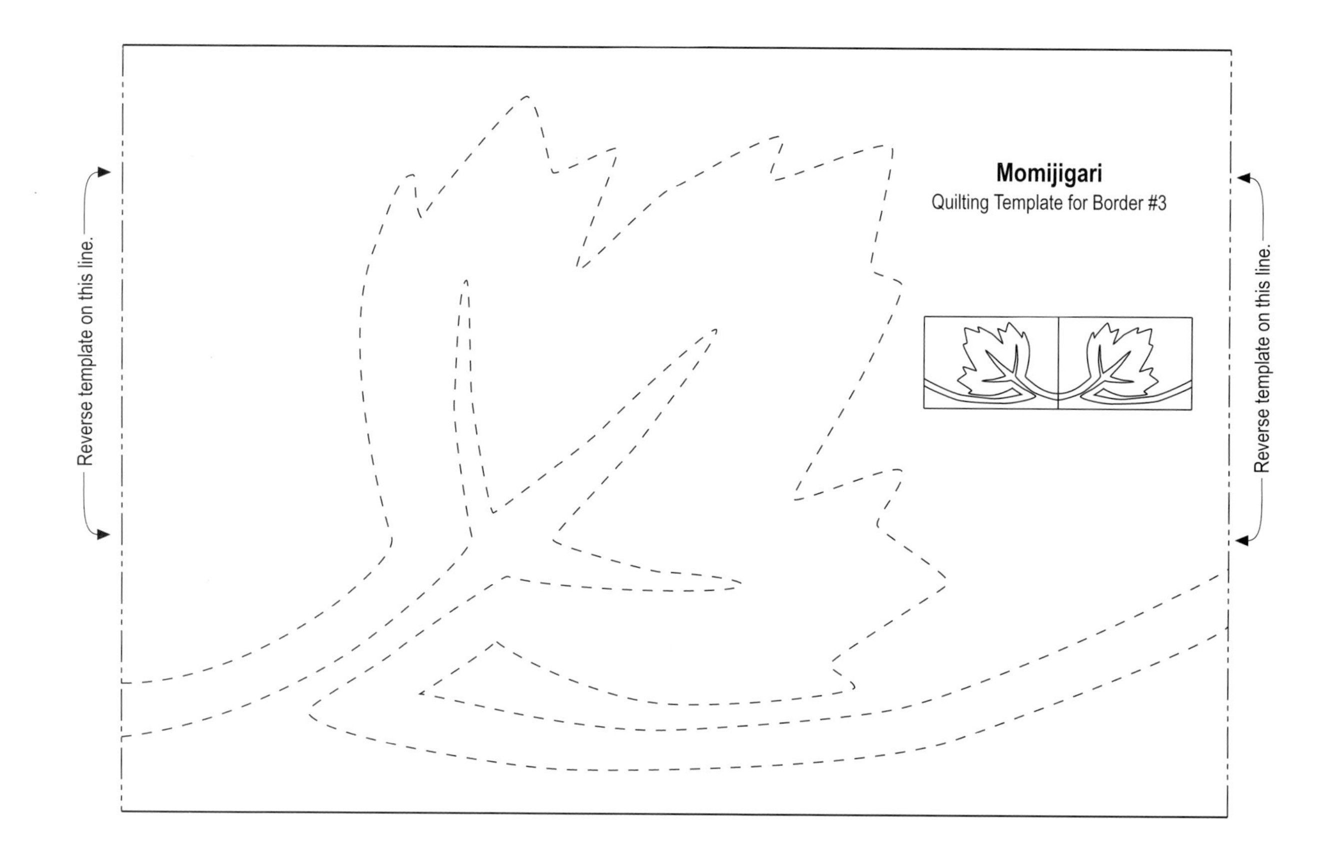
Momijigari
Quilting Template for Border #3
Reverse template on this line.
Reverse template on this line.

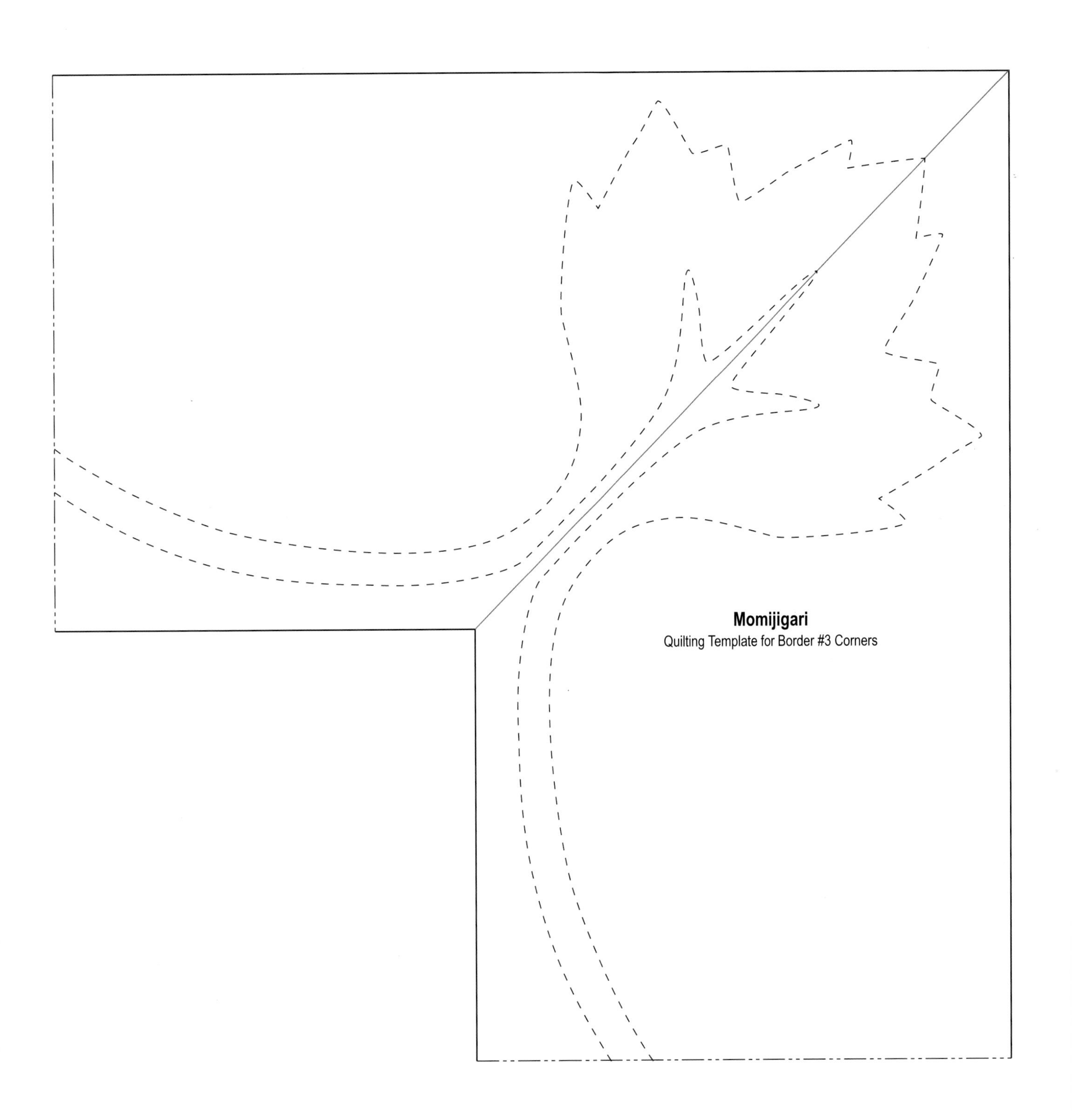
Momijigari
Quilting Template for Border #3 Corners

Take no Haru *(Bamboo Spring)*

Finished quilt size: 72" x 72"
Finished block size: 8" x 8"

In Asia, there are many species of bamboo. Japan has utilized bamboo since early times. People from the Jomon period made baskets, among other things. Being very abundant, bamboo is used in a wide variety of ways, from edible and medicinal products to household items and furniture. Japanese literature, passed down through history, includes many folk stories involving bamboo, and the "Story of the Bamboo Gatherer" has been well known for ages.

There is a form of Japanese poetry called haiku. *It consists of three lines, the first line containing five syllables; the second line, seven; and the third line, five. When expressing one's emotions in this limited format, one must choose words with careful consideration.* Take no haru, *or "Bamboo Spring," is an expression used in* haiku *to depict autumn. Bamboo sprouts come up in the spring, and by fall, the young bamboo are tall and full with beautiful green leaves. Accordingly, "Bamboo Fall" refers to spring, when the leaves fall off.*

Spring House Block

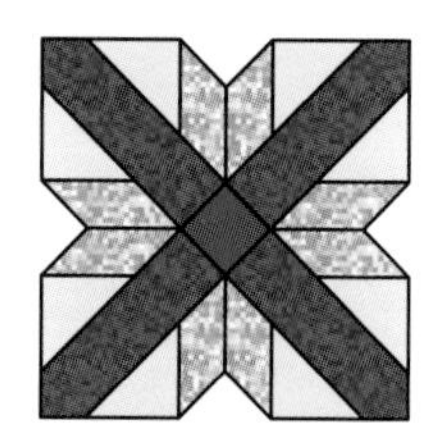

Cross Wind Block

Materials: 44"-wide fabric

Note: Kumiko Maeda selectively cut striped fabric to make all the pieces cut from one template identical. Yardage amounts given for striped fabrics do not allow for selective cutting. If you choose a striped fabric, you may need more yardage for matching, depending on the design and width of the stripe.

CROSS WIND BLOCKS

1¼ yds. gold print for diamonds A and A reversed
¾ yd. light gray print for triangle B
21½ yds. of a 2"-wide strip of dark gray stripe #1 for piece C OR 1¼ yds. dark gray print
¼ yd. emerald floral print for square D

SPRING HOUSE BLOCKS

⅜ yd. beige stripe for star points E and E reversed
⅝ yd. pink print or green-and-pink print for kite F
⅜ yd. pink stripe for triangle G
⅜ yd. emerald print for triangle H
⅜ yd. black print for square I
⅞ yd. beige print for trapezoid J and J reversed
¼ yd. purple print for triangle K
⅞ yd. medium gray print for piece L

BORDERS

⅞ yd. gold print for pieced inner and middle borders
1¼ yds. medium gray print for pieced inner border
¼ yd. light multicolored print for inner border
10 yds. of a 4"-wide purple-and-gray stripe strip for pieced inner border OR 1 yd. purple-and-gray print
8½ yds. of a 2"-wide dark gray stripe #2 strip for outer border OR ⅝ yd. dark gray print
⅝ yd. dark gray print for binding
4½ yds. for backing
82" x 82" piece of batting

Cutting

Cut all strips across the width of the fabric from selvage to selvage unless otherwise noted. Use the templates on pages 63–65.

CROSS WIND BLOCKS

From the gold print, cut:
112 *each* of diamond A and A reversed (96 each for blocks and 16 each for pieced inner border)

From the light gray print, cut:
224 triangle B (192 for blocks and 32 for pieced inner border)

From the dark gray stripe #1, cut:
128 piece C (96 for blocks and 32 for pieced inner border). *Cut each piece from the same part of the stripe.*

From the emerald floral print, cut:
40 Square D (24 for blocks and 16 for pieced inner border)

SPRING HOUSE BLOCKS

From the beige stripe, cut:
100 *each* of triangle E and E reversed

From the pink print, cut:
100 kite F

From the pink stripe, cut:
100 triangle G. *Cut each triangle from the same part of the stripe.*

From the emerald print, cut:
200 triangle H

From the black print, cut:
100 square I

From the beige print, cut:
100 *each* of trapezoid J and J reversed

From the purple print, cut:
100 triangle K

From the medium gray print, cut:
100 piece L

BORDERS

In addition to the border pieces indicated above, cut the following.

From the gold print, cut:

24 triangle N for pieced inner border

8 strips, each 2" x 42"; sew pairs of strips together end to end for middle border

12 triangle Q for pieced inner border

12 square P for pieced inner border

From the multicolored light print, cut:

12 *each* of triangle M and M reversed for pieced inner border

12 *each* of triangle O and O reversed for pieced inner border

From the purple-and-gray stripe (aligning the same stripe on each piece), cut:

12 trapezoid R for pieced inner border

4 *each* of piece S and S reversed for pieced inner border

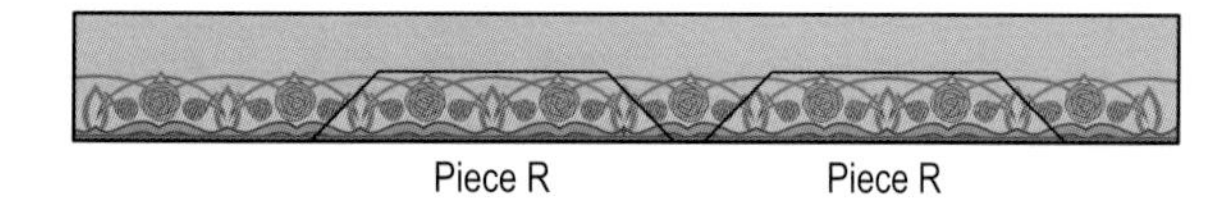

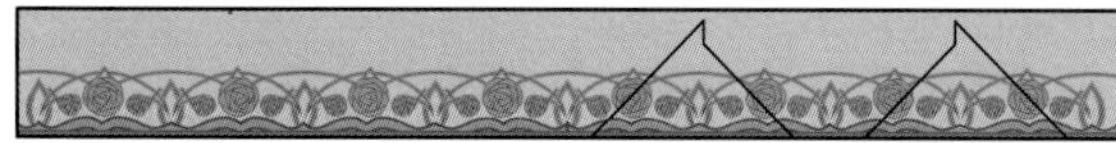

From the 2"-wide dark gray stripe #2 strip, cut:

4 segments, each 2" x 76½", for outer border

From the dark gray print, cut:

8 strips, each 1½" x 42", for binding

Block Assembly

CROSS WIND BLOCKS

1. Sew a gold print diamond A to a diamond A reversed.

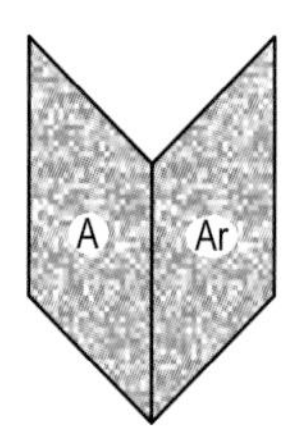

Make 112.

2. Add a light gray print triangle B to each side of each A unit. Reserve 16 A/B units to make border #2 later.

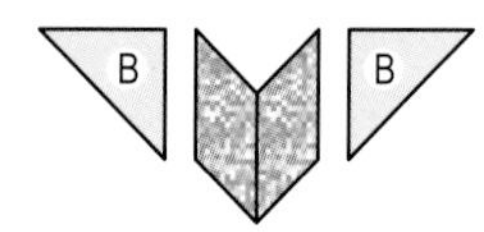

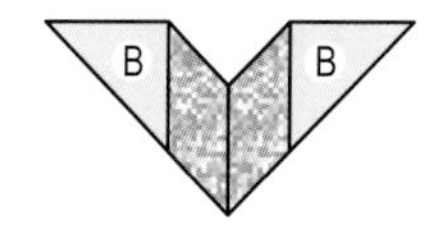

Make 112.

3. Sew a dark gray stripe piece C to opposite sides of an emerald floral print square D for the center section. Sew an A/B unit from step 2 to each side of a gray stripe piece C to complete the corner section.

Make 24.

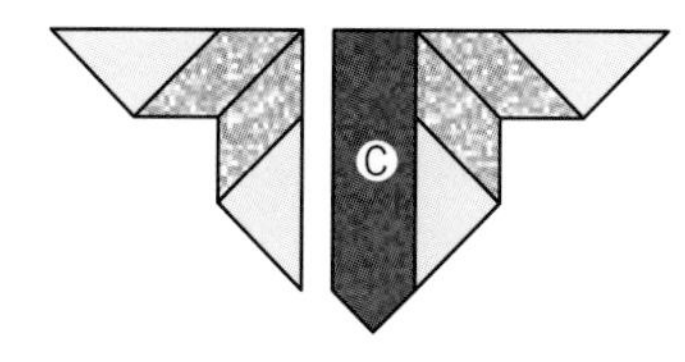

Make 48.

4. Sew a corner section to each side edge of a center section.

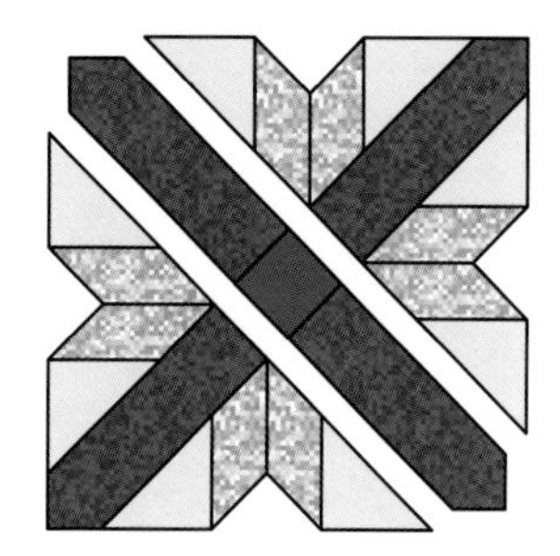

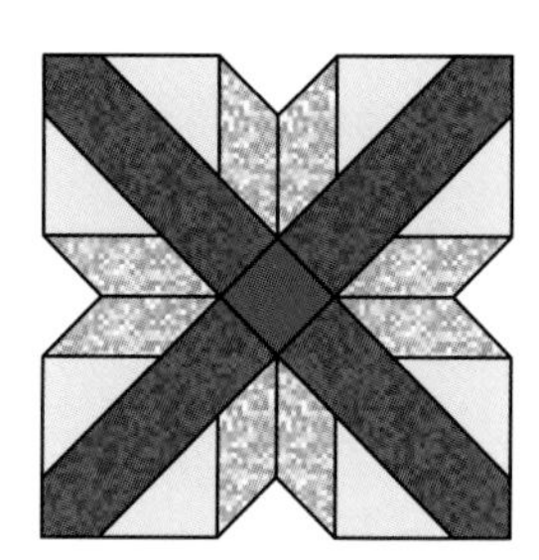

Cross Wind Block
Make 24.

SPRING HOUSE BLOCKS

1. Sew the long edge of a beige stripe triangle E and E reversed to the long edges of a kite F. Take care not to stretch the fabrics when handling bias edges.

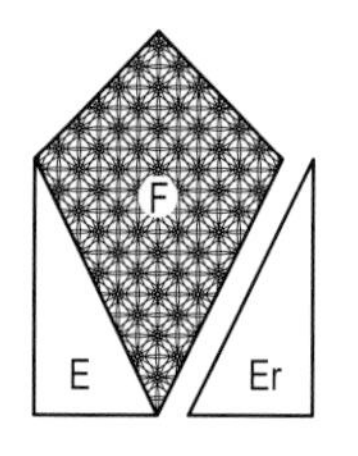

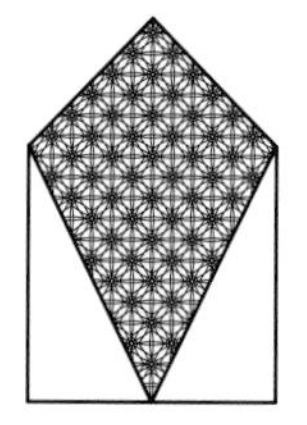

Make 100.

2. To make the center square, arrange and sew 4 pink stripe triangle G, matching the stripe.

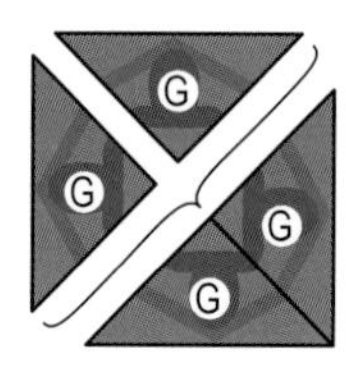

Make 25.

3. Sew an emerald triangle H to 2 adjacent edges of a black print square I.

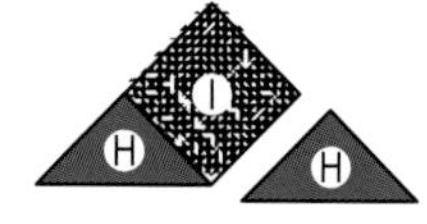

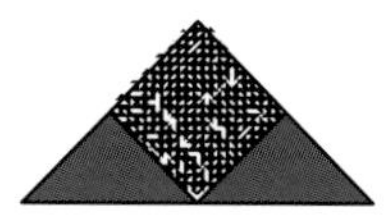

Make 100.

4. Arrange and join the units made in steps 1–3.

Spring House Block
Make 25.

5. Sew a beige print trapezoid J to a purple print triangle K; press the seam allowances toward J. Add another trapezoid J to the J/K unit, stitching in the direction indicated by the arrow. Press the seam allowances toward J (press the angled seam open if desired).

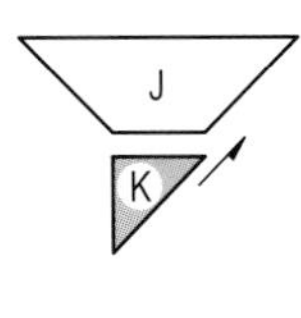

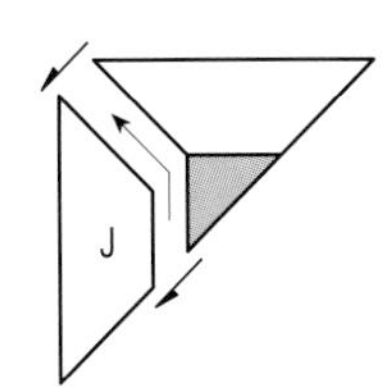

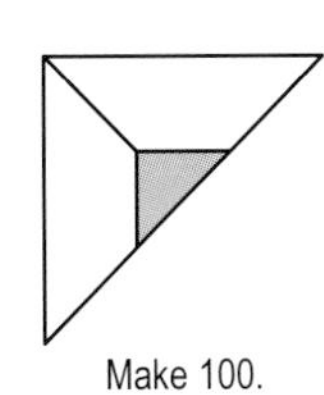

Make 100.

6. Sew a medium gray piece L to each side of the unit made in step 4, matching the centers and mitering the corners. Sew a J/K unit from step 5 to each piece L, being careful to center the units.

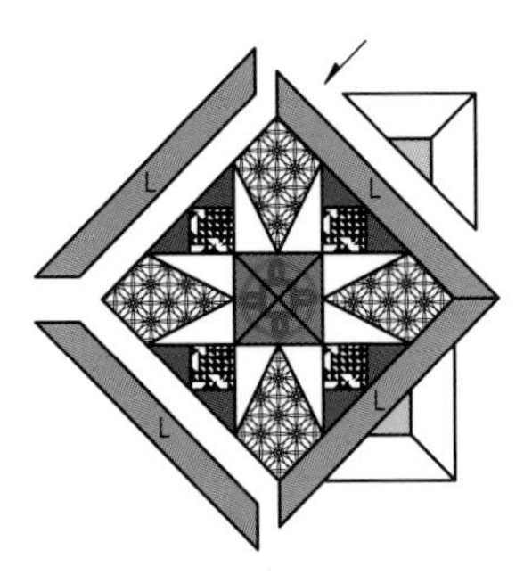

Spring House Block
Make 25.

Quilt Top Assembly

Referring to the quilt plan on page 62, arrange the Cross Wind and Spring House blocks. Place a Spring House block in each corner and alternate blocks in 7 rows of 7 blocks each. Sew the blocks together in rows, fitting the triangular extension of the Spring House block into the space in the Cross Wind block. Press the seam allowances toward the Spring House blocks. Sew the rows together.

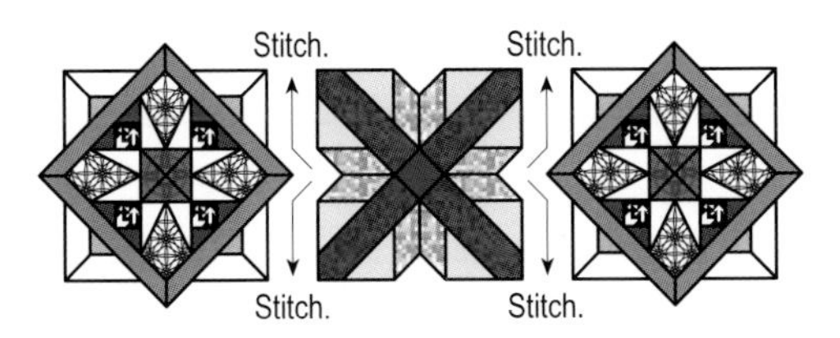

Note: If desired, stop stitching at the triangular extensions on the Spring House blocks, then appliqué the extensions last.

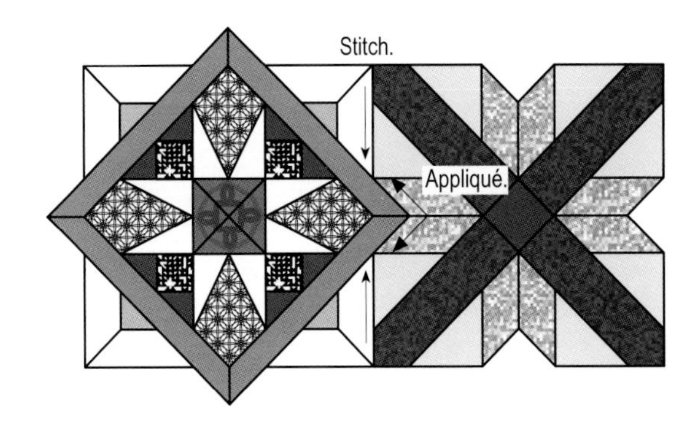

Borders

1. Sew a light multicolored print triangle M to the upper side of a gold triangle N piece; sew a triangle O to the lower side of triangle N. Repeat for triangles M and O reversed. Make 12 of each unit.

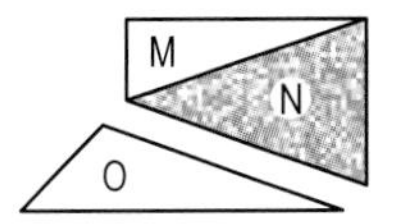

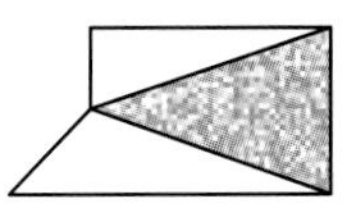

Make 12.

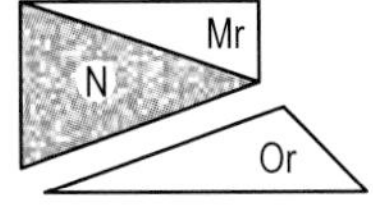

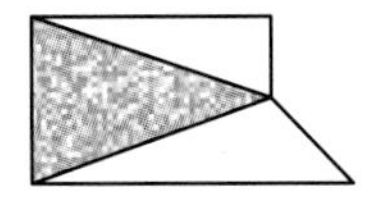

Make 12.

2. Sew an M/N/O unit to the left edge of a medium gray square P; sew the M/N/O reverse unit to the opposite edge of the same square. Add a medium gray triangle Q to the top edge of square P.

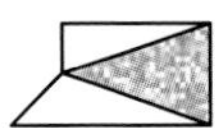
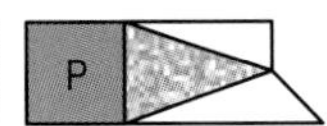

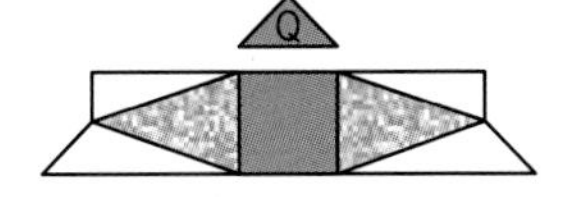

Make 12.

3. Add a purple-and-gray stripe trapezoid R to each unit to complete border unit #1.

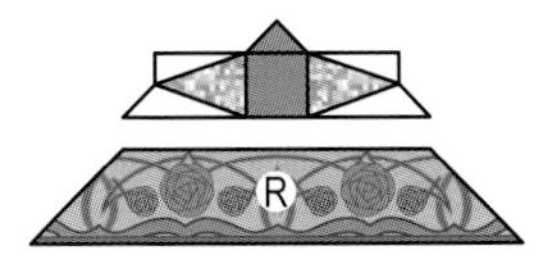

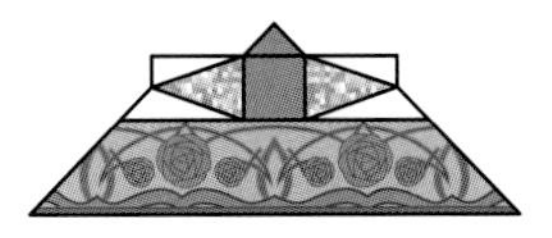

Border Unit #1
Make 12.

4. Sew a piece C to each of the 16 Cross Wind A/B units made in step 2 on page 60. Sew a square D to one end of a piece C and add it to the pieced unit to make border unit #2.

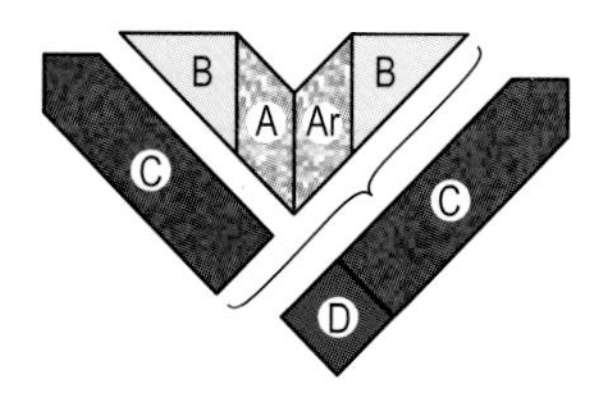

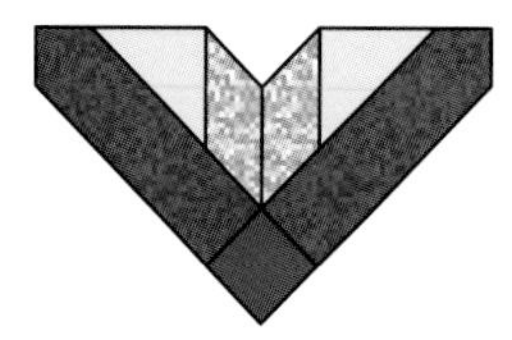

Border Unit #2
Make 16.

5. Arrange and join 3 border unit #1 and 4 border unit #2 to construct the pieced inner border. Add a corner piece S to the left end and an S reversed to the right end of each pieced inner border strip.

Inner Pieced Border
Make 4.

6. Add an inner pieced border strip to each edge of the quilt top. Do not miter the corner seams yet.

7. Referring to steps 7–9 of "Borders" for "Bingatazome" on page 17, match the border centers, sewing a 2"-wide gold middle border strip to each pieced inner border, then adding a 2"-wide dark gray stripe #2 outer border strip to each middle border strip. Miter the corners of all 3 borders, treating them as one unit. Trim the seam allowances to ¼"; press the seams open.

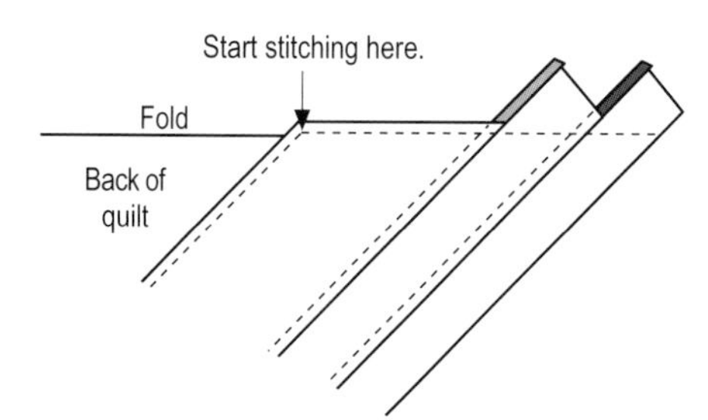

Finishing

1. Press the quilt top, pressing the border seam allowances toward the outer edges.
2. Layer the quilt top with batting and backing; baste.
3. Quilt as desired.
4. Bind the edges.

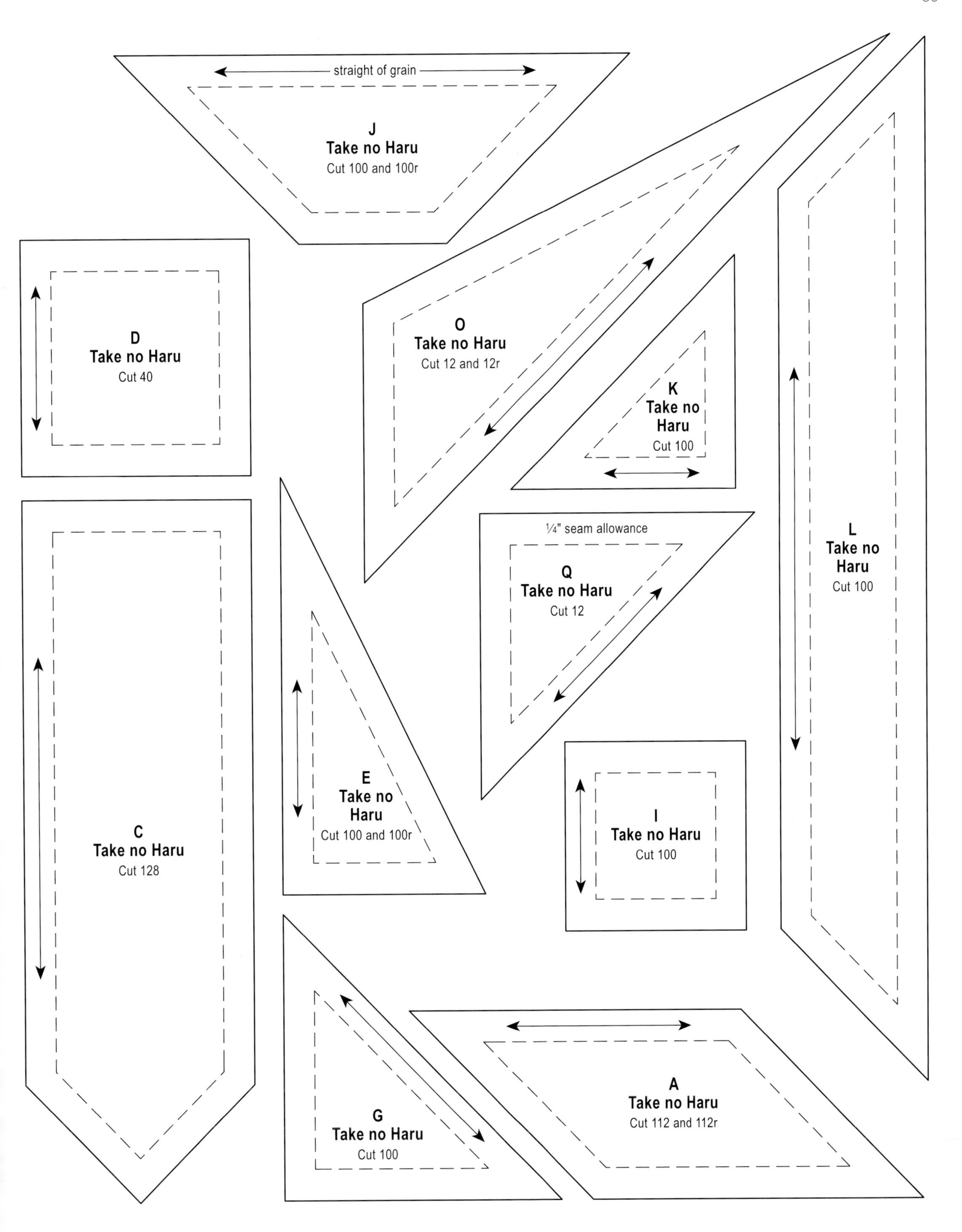
straight of grain
J
Take no Haru
Cut 100 and 100r
D
Take no Haru
Cut 40
O
Take no Haru
Cut 12 and 12r
K
Take no
Haru
Cut 100
L
Take no
Haru
Cut 100
¼" seam allowance
Q
Take no Haru
Cut 12
C
Take no Haru
Cut 128
E
Take no
Haru
Cut 100 and 100r
I
Take no Haru
Cut 100
G
Take no Haru
Cut 100
A
Take no Haru
Cut 112 and 112r

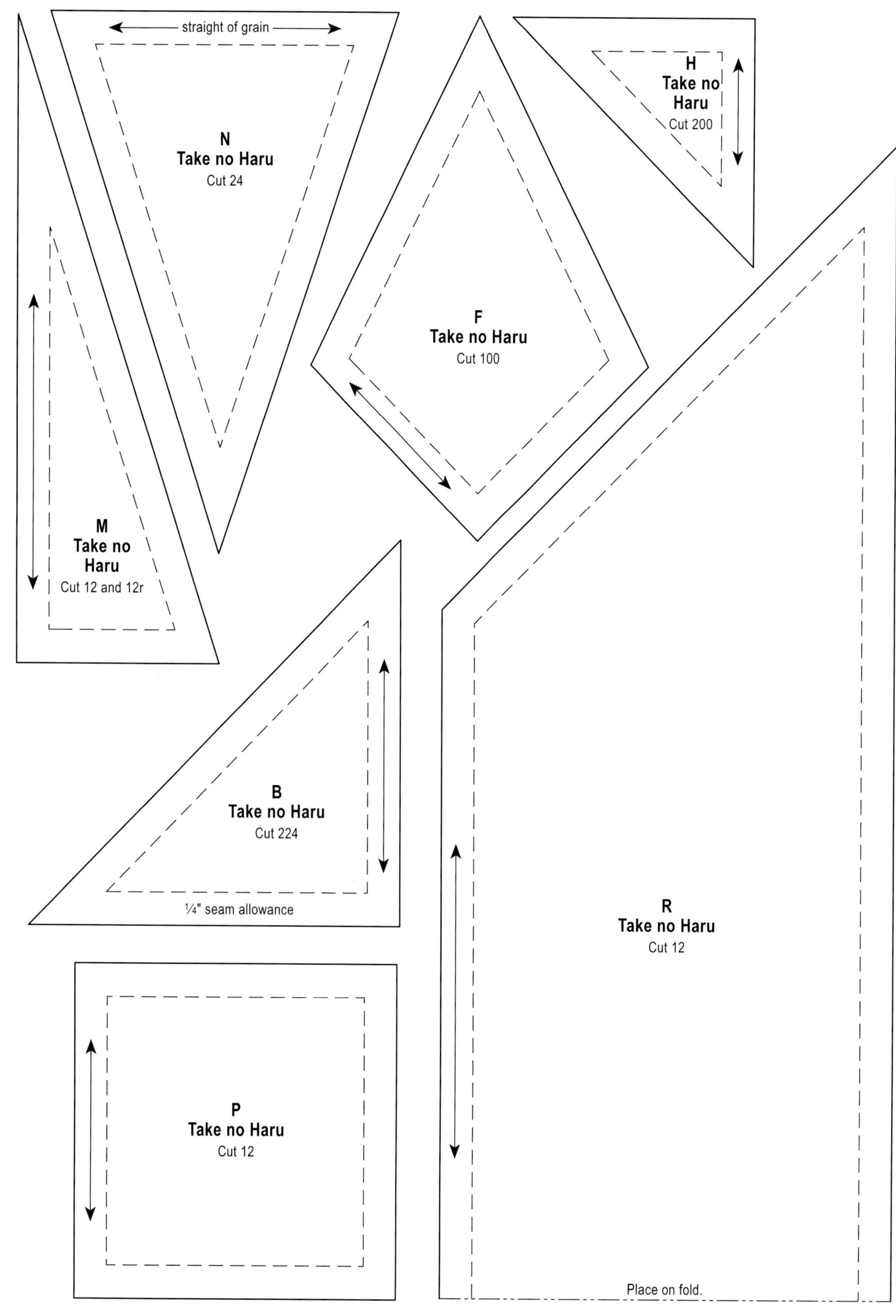
straight of grain
N
Take no Haru
Cut 24
F
Take no Haru
Cut 100
H
Take no
Haru
Cut 200
M
Take no
Haru
Cut 12 and 12r
B
Take no Haru
Cut 224
¼" seam allowance
R
Take no Haru
Cut 12
Place on fold.
P
Take no Haru
Cut 12

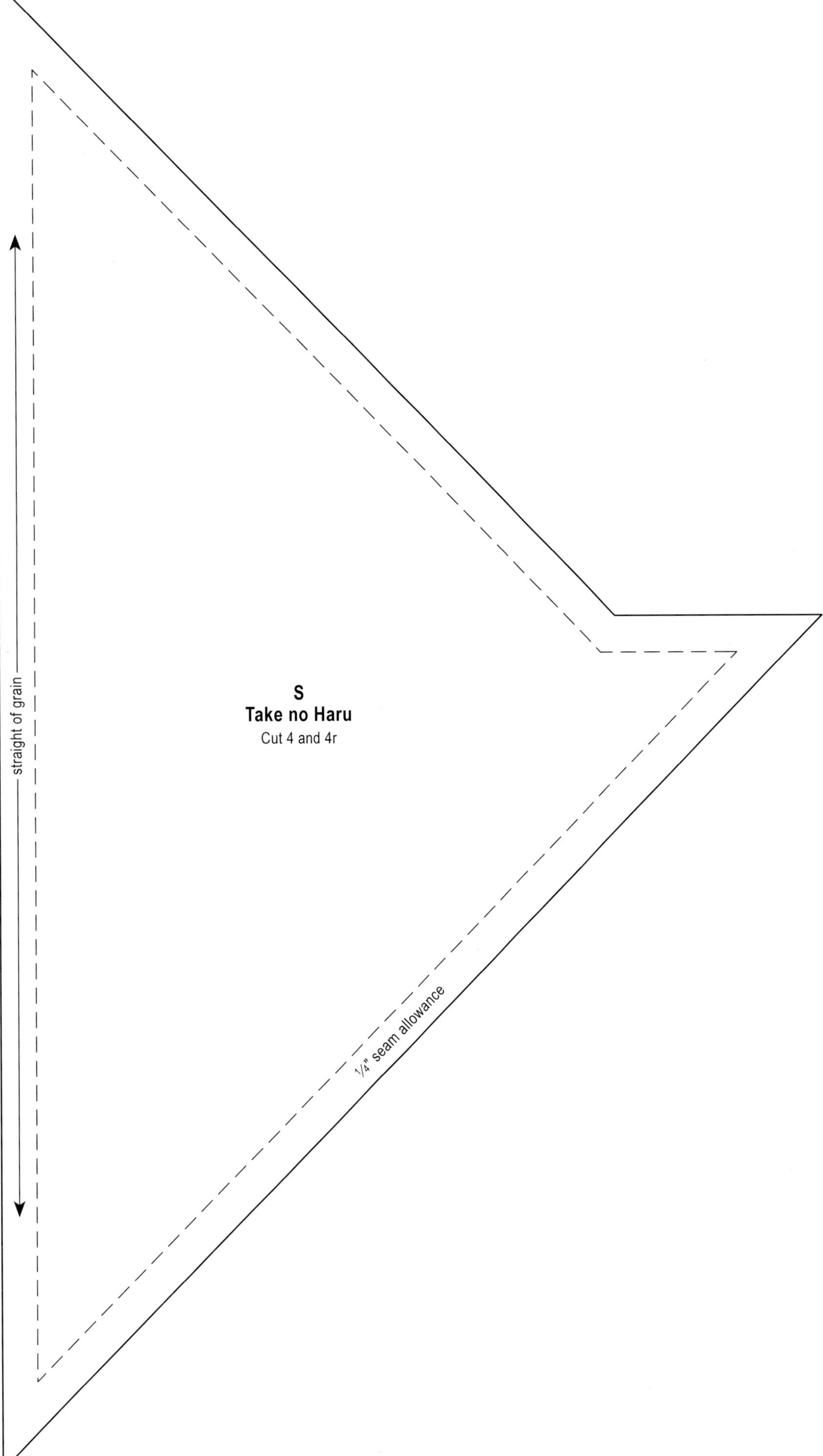
S
Take no Haru
Cut 4 and 4r
straight of grain
¼" seam allowance

Akinoyonaga *(Long Autumn Nights)*

Finished quilt size: 29" x 29"

During the long nights toward the end of autumn, when the flowers are gone, I often ponder the blossoms of the four seasons while making quilts. The Shiki no Hana *(Flowers of Four Seasons) motif is often seen in Japanese interior and* kimono *designs. Its depiction of the four seasons makes it appropriate at any time of year. The plum blossoms represent spring; the iris and flowing stream, summer; the chrysanthemum and red leaves, autumn; and the bamboo leaves, winter. The fan shapes in this quilt are called* suehiro, *because of the V-shaped design.* Suehiro *is considered a symbol of good luck.*

Mariko Miwa attached four knotted cords to each corner of her quilt. Instructions for these decorative knots are included, but feel free to use your own ideas to make this project original and fun.

Materials: 44"-wide fabric

20½" x 20½" square of light gray print for background
⅞ yd. black print for background and outer border
⅛ yd. dark red–and-black print for sashing
5 assorted pink print rectangles, each 3" x 5", for plum blossoms
1 brown print rectangle, 6" x 15", for plum branch
7 assorted yellow print squares, each 4" x 4", for butterfly and iris blossoms
3 assorted yellow-green print rectangles, each 3" x 11", for bamboo leaves
8 assorted green print scraps in various sizes for leaves
3 assorted light blue print squares, each 10" x 10", for stream
2 purple print squares, each 4" x 4", for iris
1 purple print and 1 red print square, each 4" x 4", for chrysanthemums
1 mustard yellow print rectangle, 2" x 4", for chrysanthemum centers
3 assorted rust print squares, each 5" x 5", for maple leaves
33 assorted strips, each 1½" x 3", for fans (such as pink, yellow, purple, red, green, and mauve)
4 scraps, each 3" x 3", for corner fan centers
1⅜ yds. red-and-black plaid for backing and binding
Red, green, lavender, and yellow embroidery floss for *sashiko* sections
Gold metallic thread
35 gold metallic seed beads for plum blossoms
80" (2¼ yds.) of red braid or cord for corners of fans
35" x 35" piece of batting

Cutting

Cut all strips across the width of the fabric from selvage to selvage unless otherwise noted.

From the black print, cut:
1 square, 20½" x 20½", for background
4 rectangles, each 4½" x 20½", for border
4 squares, each 4½" x 4½", for corners

From the dark red–and-black print, cut:
2 strips, each 1" x 20½", for sashing
4 strips, each 1" x 4½", for sashing
2 strips, each 1" x 29½", for sashing

From the red-and-black plaid, cut:
1 square, 35" x 35", for backing
4 strips, each 1½" wide, for binding

Assembly

1. Using a removable-ink marking pen or pencil, draw a circle on the light gray background print. Do not cut out the circle until appliqué is complete. Refer to the pullout pattern for the placement diagram and appliqué patterns.

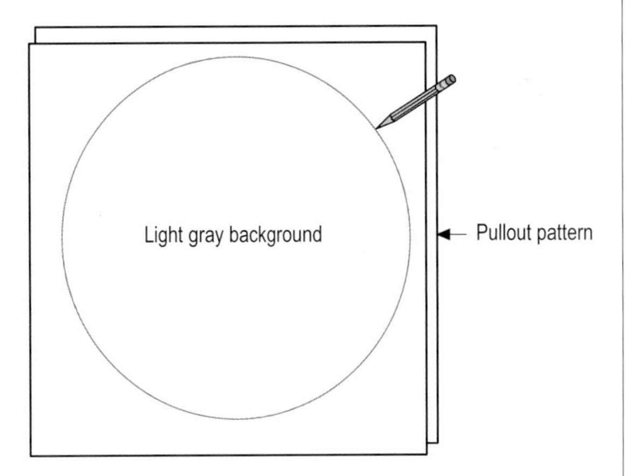

2. Trace patterns for appliqué, referring to the placement diagram. Cut out each fabric piece, adding a scant ¼"-wide seam allowance. Prepare all pieces for appliqué, using your favorite method.
3. Beginning with the spring section, appliqué plum branches #1 and #2, and flowers and buds #3–#20. Appliqué the winter section, including bamboo leaves #21–#27.

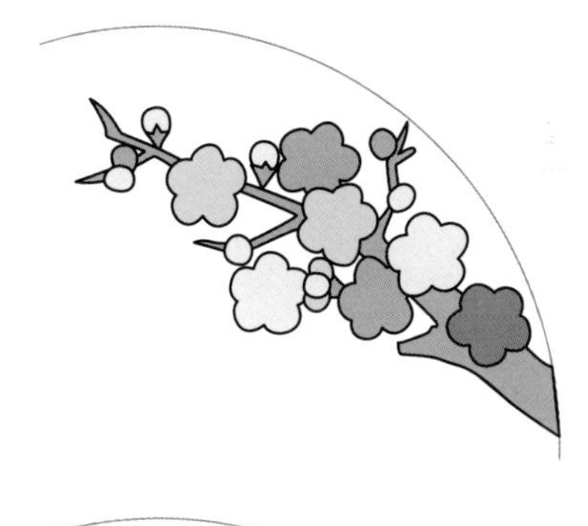

4. Appliqué the summer section, starting with the stream (sections A, B, and C) in numerical order. Leave stream piece #3b open where it will overlap the iris stems.

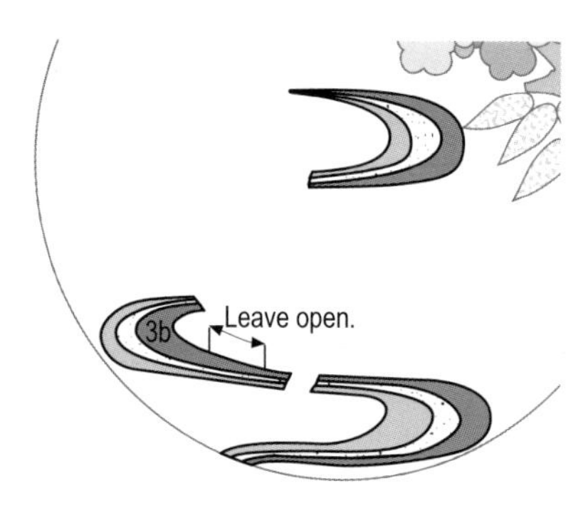

5. Appliqué iris leaves #1–#7; then finish appliquéing piece #3b. Appliqué iris petals #8–#15 and #16–#23. Appliqué butterfly pieces #1–#7.

6. Appliqué the fall section, starting with chrysanthemum leaves #1–#5. Appliqué chrysanthemum petals #6–#9, and maple leaves #10–#12.

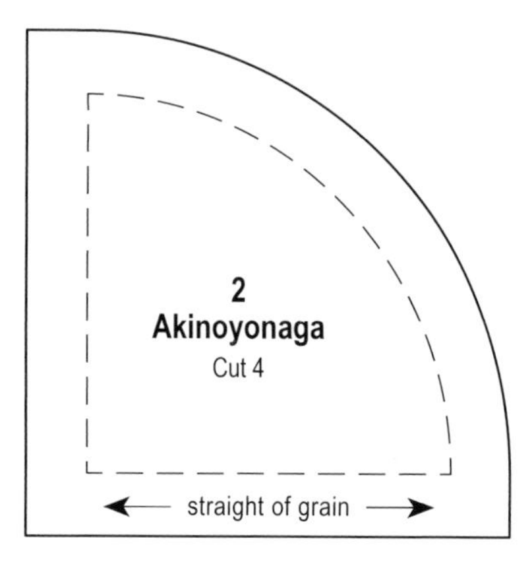

7. Embroider the butterfly's antennae.
8. Cut out the appliquéd circle, leaving a ¼"-wide seam allowance. Appliqué the circle to the 20½" x 20½" black square.

9. Cut away the black fabric behind the appliquéd circle, being careful not to cut through to the front. This way, the black fabric won't show through the light gray circle.
10. Cut fan piece #1 from each of the assorted 1½" x 3" strips. For each corner, sew 6 fan segments together. Using fan Template #2, cut 4 fan centers. Appliqué a center to each 6-segment fan. Appliqué each fan to a 4½" black square.

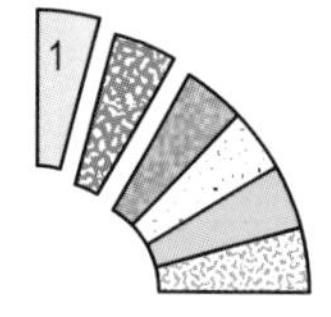

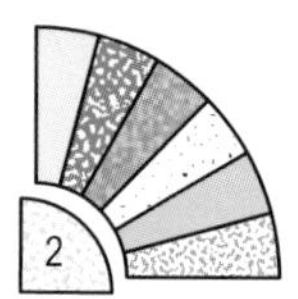

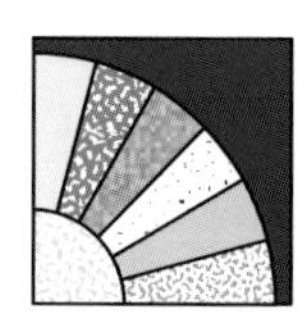

Appliquéd Fan Block
Make 4.

11. Sew fan segments (piece #1) together as shown to make the remaining folded fans. Set aside the 2 remaining segments. Appliqué them to the quilt after adding the borders.

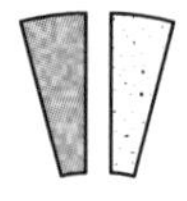
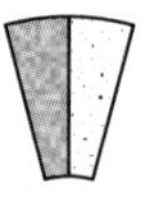

Make 2.

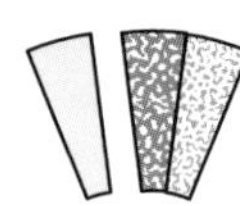
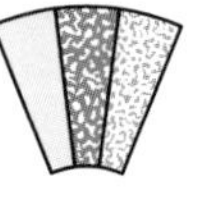

Make 1.

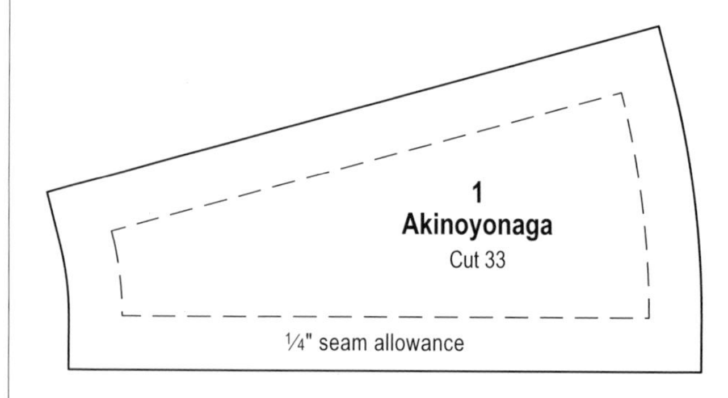

Borders

1. Sew a 1" x 20½" dark red–and-black print strip, then a 4½" x 20½" black rectangle to each side of the quilt top.

2. Sew a 1" x 4½" dark red–and-black print strip to each end of the 2 remaining 4½" x 20½" black rectangles, then sew an appliquéd fan block to each dark red–and-black strip.

3. Sew a 1" x 29½" dark red–and-black print strip, then a border strip made in step 2 to the top and bottom edges of the quilt top, orienting the fans as shown.

4. Position and appliqué the folded fan segments from step 11 on page 68 to the quilt top. Choose your own pleasing arrangement, keeping in mind the overall balance, or refer to the quilt plan on page 70 for placement.

Finishing

1. Layer the quilt top with batting and backing; baste.
2. Quilt as desired. Mariko Miwa echo-quilted the black corners of the center section, then quilted swirls in the light gray circle to represent the flowing stream.

With metallic thread, Mariko quilted the center of each fan segment, using a backstitch and extending the line on the folded fans to form a handle.

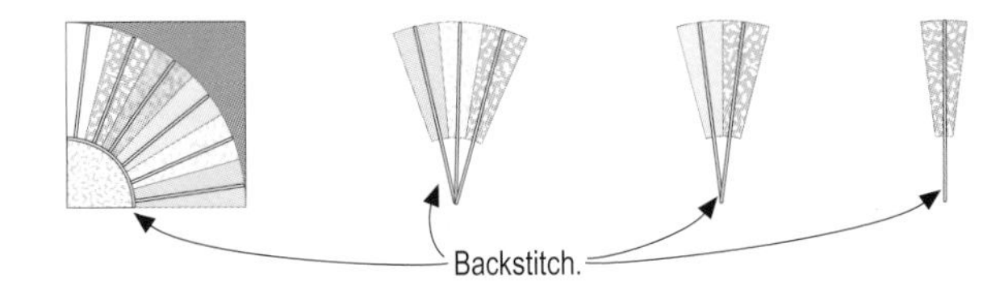

3. Quilt the outer borders using *sashiko* designs and stitching. Divide the borders into 4 sections and stitch a different design in each section. Copy the designs on page 71, or choose your own design. Use the red, green, lavender, and yellow embroidery floss for the *sashiko* running stitch, using 1 color for each section.

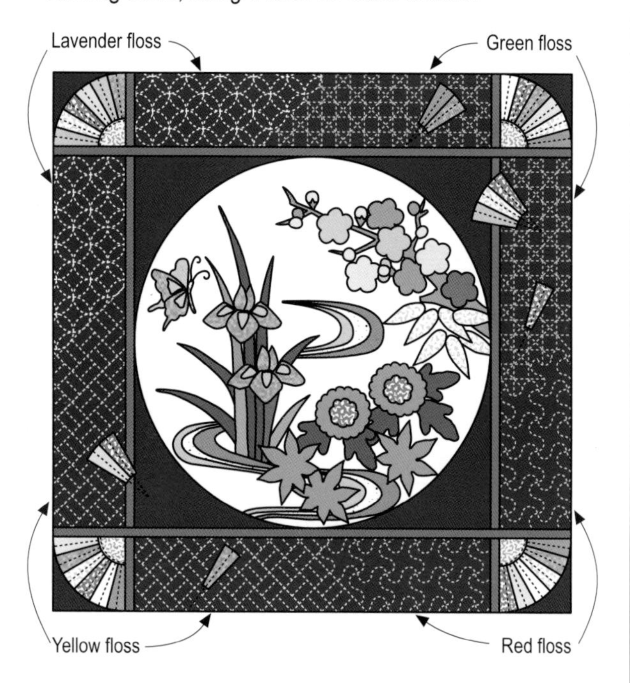

4. With gold metallic thread, make 5 straight stitches at the center of each plum blossom. Attach a gold bead at the outer end of each stitch.

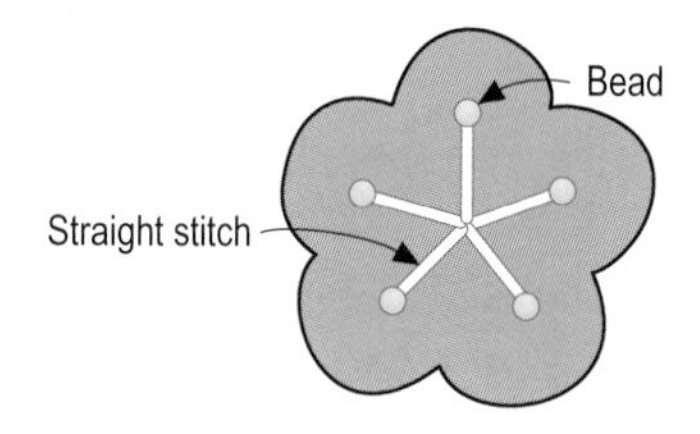

5. Bind the edges.

6. Cut the red braid or cord into 4 pieces, each 20" long. Tie each cord into a decorative knot, following the diagrams below. Attach the knotted cord to the inside corner of each Fan block.

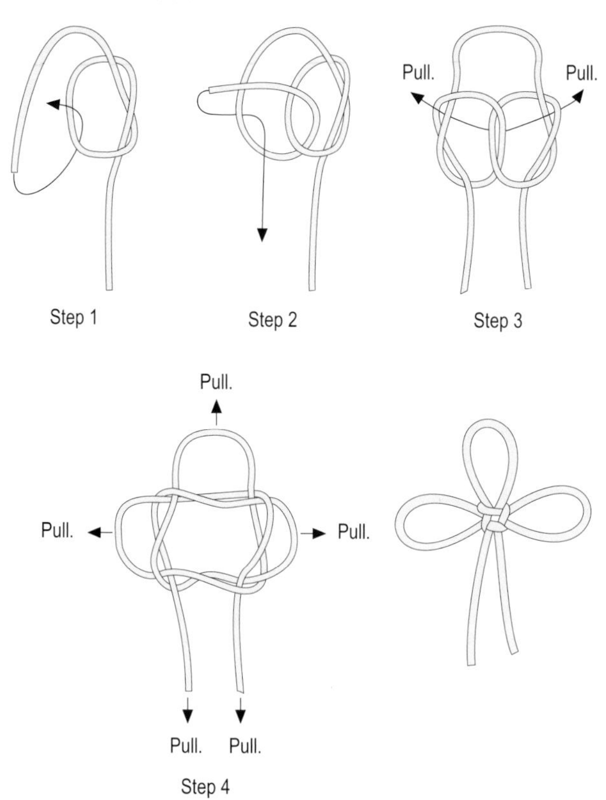

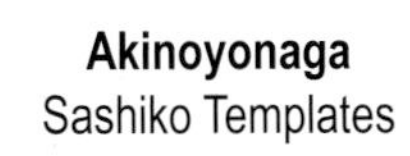

Akinoyonaga
Sashiko Templates

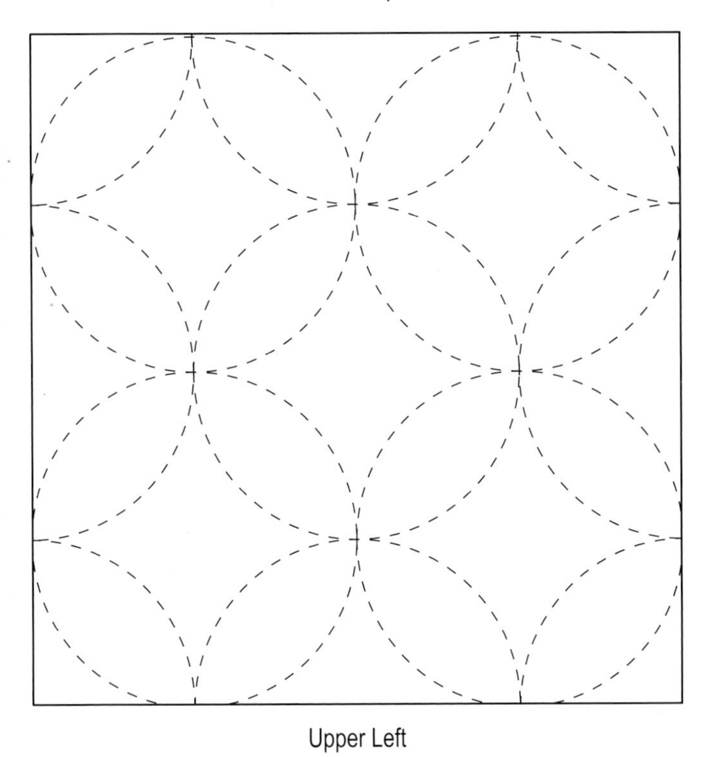

Upper Left

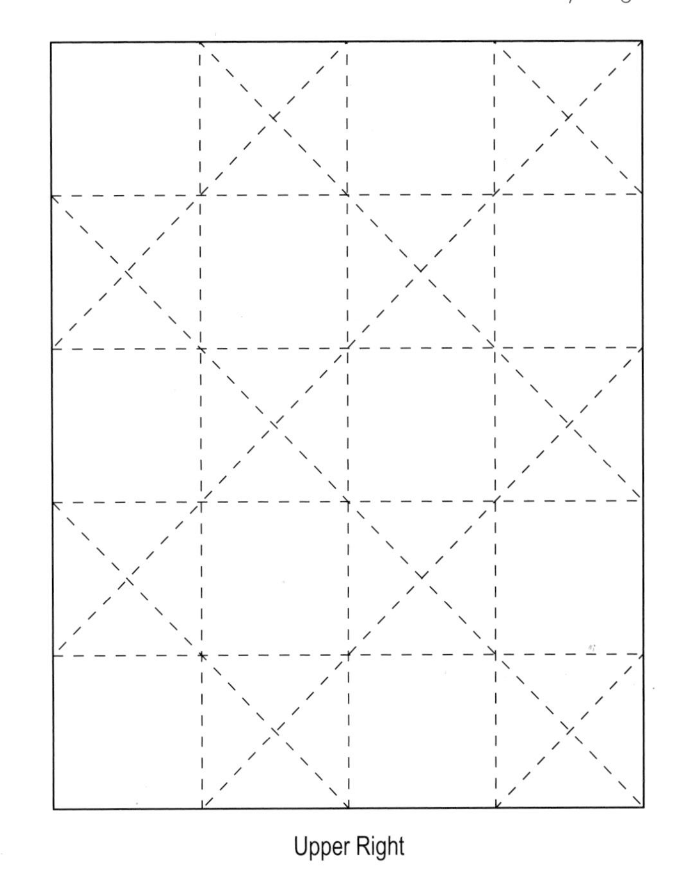

Upper Right

Lower Left

Lower Right

◀ Kazaguruma
(Pinwheel)
by Takako Onoyama

▼ Kinkakuji
(Golden Temple) by
Kazuko Wada

Kamon ▶
(Family Crest)
by Takako Onoyama

▼ Hatsu Haru
(New Year's Day)
by Takako Onoyama

Kazaguruma *(Pinwheel)*

Finished quilt size: 28½" x 33"

Finished block size: 2¼" x 2¼"

Pinwheels were first brought to Japan from China about one thousand years ago. During the Edo period, pinwheels were adopted as New Year's toys. Many people brought them home as souvenirs when visiting temples during the New Year's celebration. In addition to paper, pinwheels are also made of thin strips of wood. They are a popular form of folk art, although most of the pinwheels sold today are made of plastic. In this quilt, I wanted to express my childhood memories of paper pinwheels printed with beautiful kimono *designs.*

Although children's toys differ in design and color, toys all over the world have many things in common. It intrigues me that whether they are dolls, stuffed animals, games, moving toys, or pinwheels, they all say something about the culture they come from. I hope this remains unchanged.

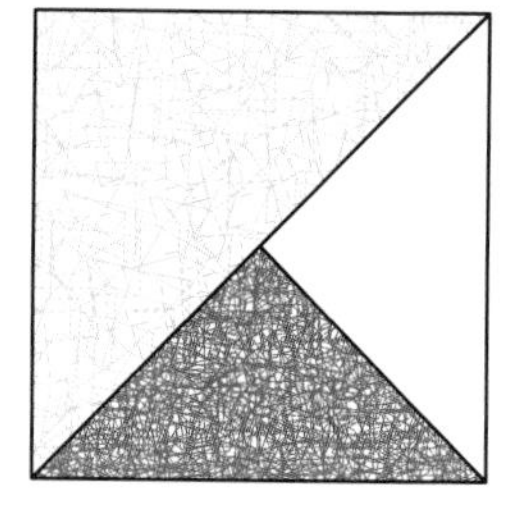

Materials: 44"-wide fabric

½ yd. *total* assorted red prints
½ yd. *total* assorted blue prints
½ yd. *total* assorted light pink prints
½ yd. *total* assorted light blue prints
1 yd. *total* assorted beige-and-white prints
⅜ yd. medium gray print for outer border
¼ yd. dark blue print for inner border
1 yd. for backing
32" x 36" piece of batting

Cutting

Cut all strips across the width of the fabric from selvage to selvage unless otherwise noted.

Note: Use the triangle templates on page 77. If you wish to speed-cut these triangles, first cut squares, then cut the squares diagonally.

For the large triangles, cut the squares 3⅛" x 3⅛", then cut the squares once diagonally to make 2 triangles.

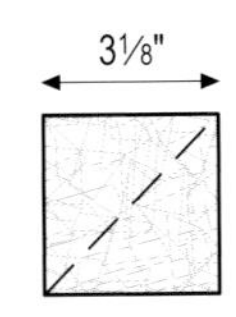

Large Triangles

For the small triangles, cut the squares 3½" x 3½", then cut the squares twice diagonally to make 4 triangles.

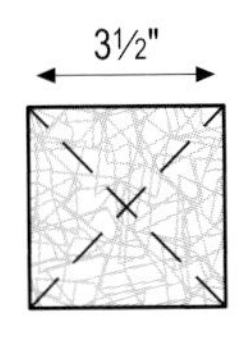

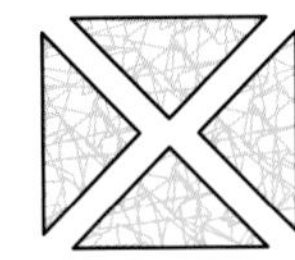

Small Triangles

From the assorted red prints, cut a total of:
- 36 large triangles
- 36 small triangles

From the assorted blue prints, cut a total of:
- 16 large triangles
- 20 small triangles

From the assorted light pink prints, cut a total of:
- 26 large triangles
- 24 small triangles

From the assorted light blue prints, cut a total of:
- 42 large triangles
- 54 small triangles

From the assorted beige-and-white prints, cut a total of:
- 110 small triangles

From the medium gray print, cut:
- 4 strips, each 2¾" wide, for outer border

From the dark blue print, cut:
- 4 strips, each 1" wide, for inner border

Assembly

1. Following the diagram for color placement and numbers of blocks, sew 2 small triangles together, then sew this unit to a large triangle to make each 2¾" x 2¾" block. You will have 2 small beige-and-white and 2 small red triangles remaining.

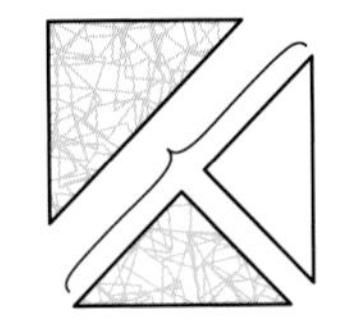

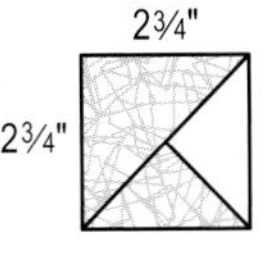

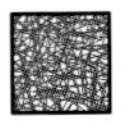
Red prints

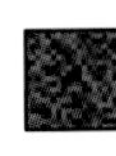
Blue prints

Light pink prints

Light blue prints

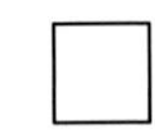
Beige-and-white prints

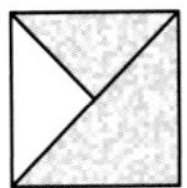
A
Make 38.

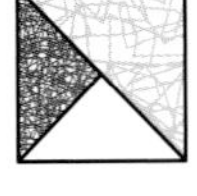
B
Make 6.

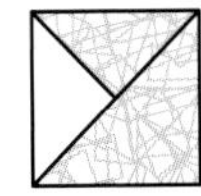
C
Make 16.

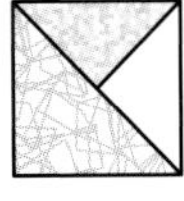
D
Make 1.

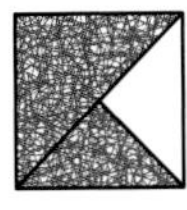
E
Make 24.

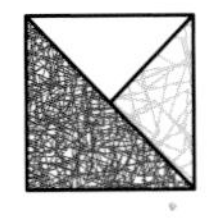
F
Make 4.

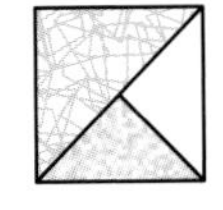
G
Make 3.

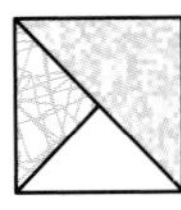
H
Make 4.

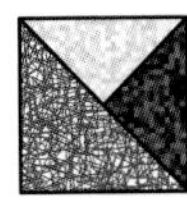
I
Make 4.

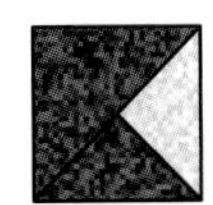
J
Make 8.

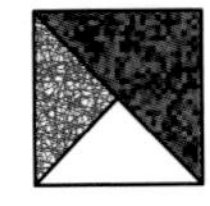
K
Make 4.

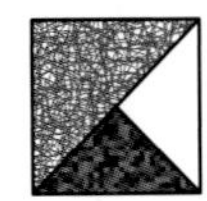
L
Make 4.

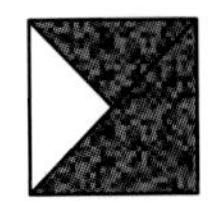
M
Make 4.

2. Following the placement diagram below, arrange the blocks, being careful to orient large and small triangles as shown.

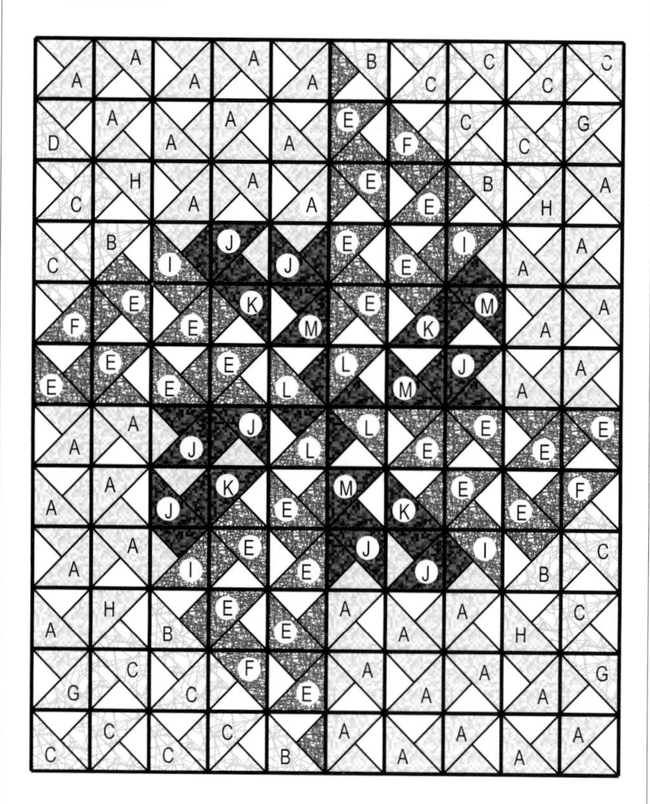

3. Sew the blocks together in rows of 5 blocks each. Press seam allowances toward the large triangles. Sew the rows into quadrants, then sew the quadrants together.

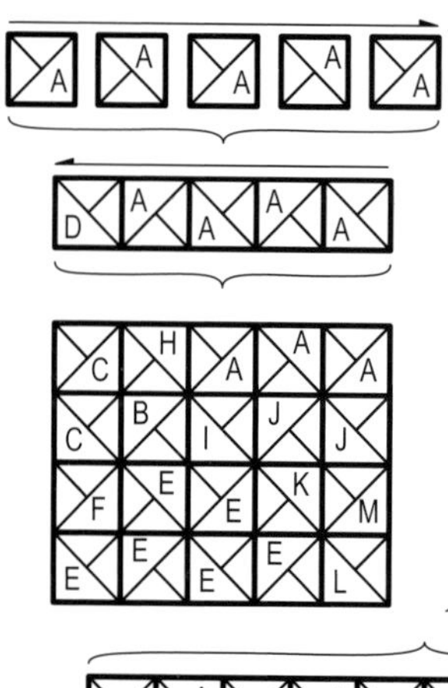

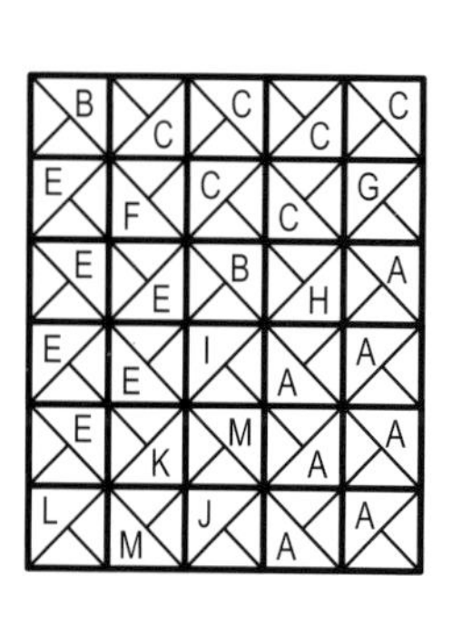

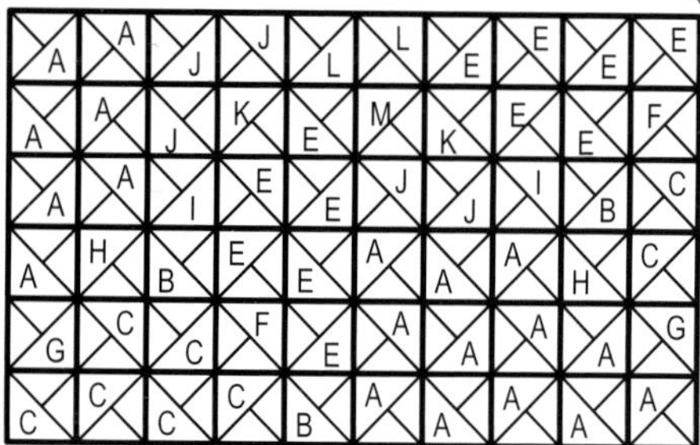

Borders

1. Sew a small beige-and-white triangle to each remaining small red triangle as shown.

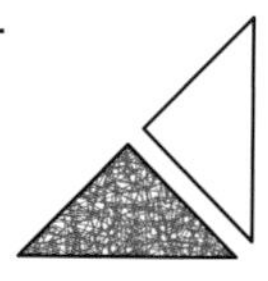

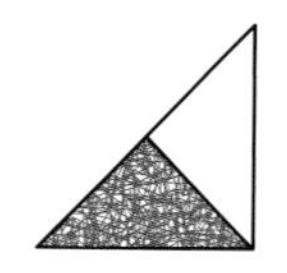

Make 2.

2. Sew a 1"-wide dark blue strip to each 2¾"-wide medium gray strip to make 4 pieced border strips. Cut 2 of the border strips in half crosswise. Cut the end of 2 of the half strips at a 45° angle as shown.

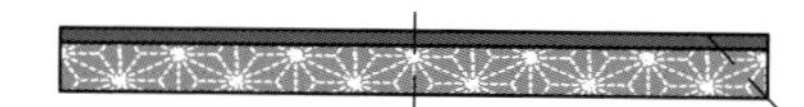

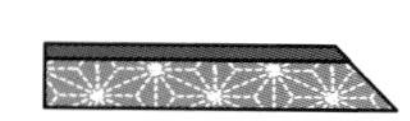

Make 2.

3. Sew a triangle unit made in step 1 to the angled end of each half strip. Make sure the beige-and-white triangle is next to the dark blue strip. Sew the remaining half strip to the red triangle as shown to make the pieced border.

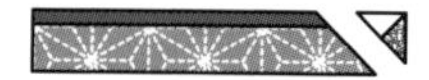

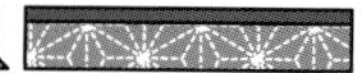

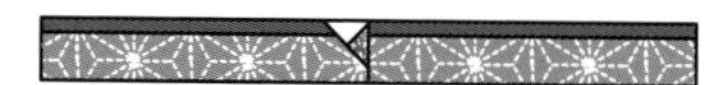

Make 2.

4. Sew the pieced borders to the sides of the quilt top with the dark blue strips next to the edges of the quilt top. Align the triangle unit with block E on both sides. Press the seam allowances toward the borders.

5. Sew the remaining pieced border strips to the top and bottom of the quilt top; miter the corners.

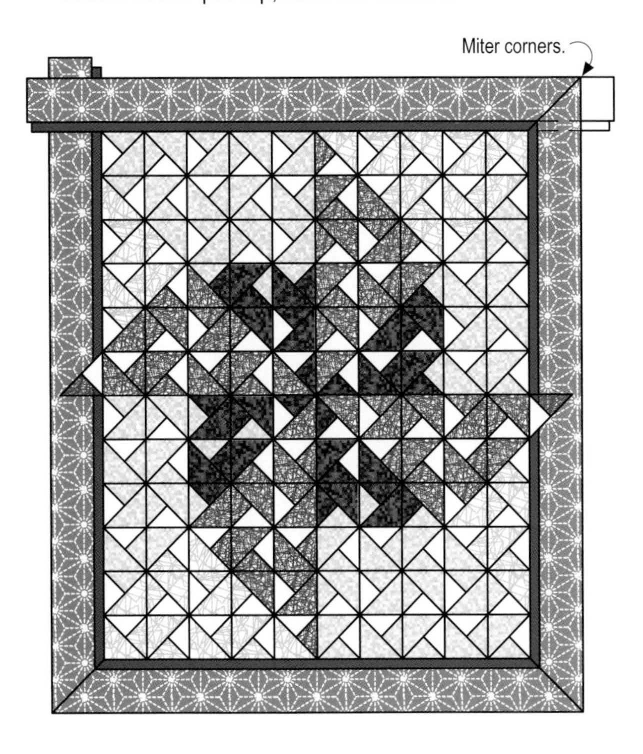

Finishing

1. Layer the quilt top with batting and backing; baste.
2. Quilt as desired, quilting to within ½" from the outer edges of the quilt top.
3. Trim the edges of the quilt top, batting, and backing so they are even. Trim an additional ¼" from the batting so the top and backing extend ¼" beyond the batting. Turn under ¼" of the raw edges of both the quilt top and the backing; align the edges and pin or baste. Whipstitch the top and backing together.

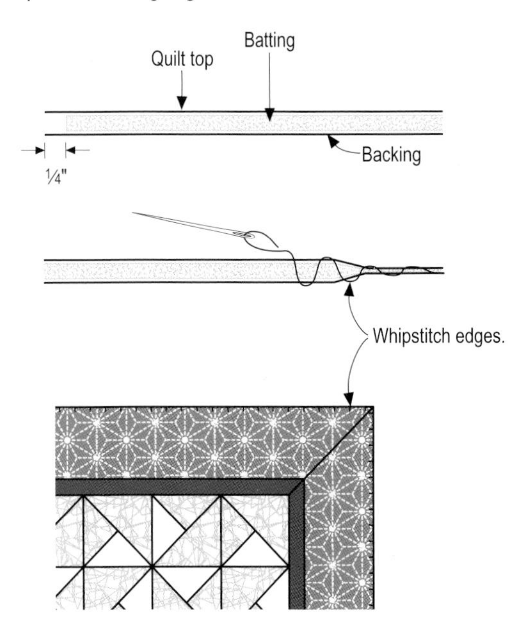

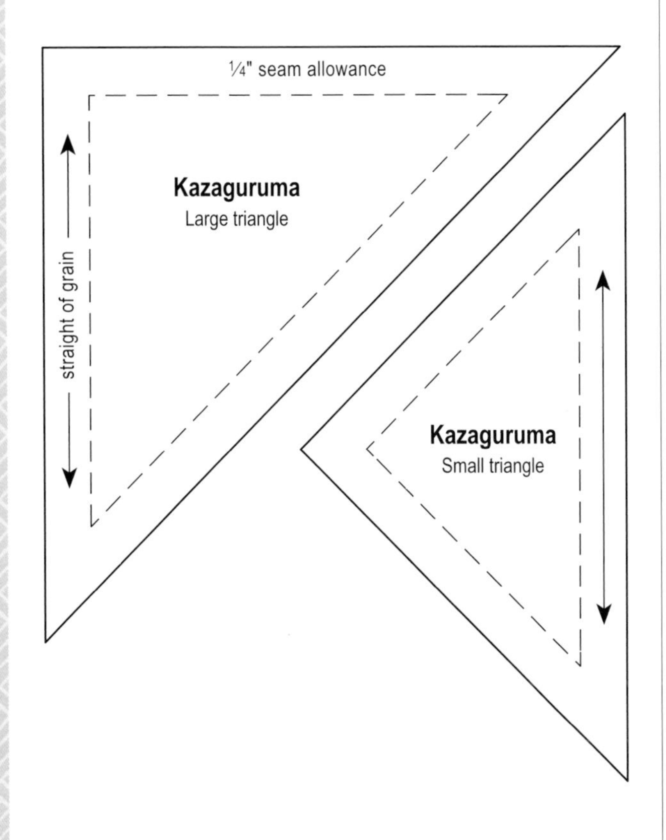

Kinkakuji *(Golden Temple)*

Finished quilt size: 61" x 61"

In the northern part of Kyoto, there is a famous temple that was constructed more than six hundred years ago. The exterior of the three-story building is covered in gold leaf; the interior design varies from floor to floor. Inside the main temple, a breathtaking garden—made over many years through the harmonious energies of man and nature—includes pine trees, a moss garden, and a rock garden. The image of the temple, Kinkakuji, reflected in the nearby pond, changes with the seasons along with the surrounding trees. The scene keeps the steady stream of tourists entranced.

The center design of this quilt represents the temple, and the borders refer to the surrounding gardens.

Materials: 44"-wide fabric

3⅓ yds. yellow border print for blocks and borders
1¼ yds. beige print #1 for background
¾ yd. blue print for blocks, third border, and binding
⅝ yd. *total* of 4 assorted yellow prints, ranging in value from light to dark, for blocks and borders
½ yd. large-scale green-and-rust print for blocks and borders
⅛ yd. small-scale rust print for blocks
⅝ yd. large-scale gold-and-blue print for blocks and borders
½ yd. beige print #2 for third border
3⅞ yds. for backing
65" x 65" piece of batting

Cutting

Cut all strips across the width of the fabric from selvage to selvage unless otherwise noted. Use the templates on pages 84–86 and on the pullout.

Note: For several of the templates, Kazuko Wada cut identical pieces from the border fabric's design. Yardage amounts given for fabrics do not allow for this selective cutting. If you choose a striped fabric, you may need more yardage, depending upon the design and width of the stripe.

From different "stripes" of the yellow border print, cut:

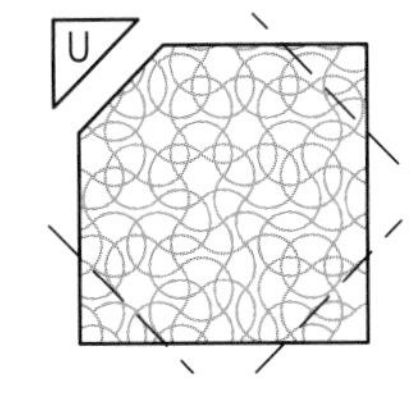

1 square, 6¼" x 6¼", for Feathered Star center. Trim each corner to make an octagon, using Cutting Template U on page 86.
8 kite A for Feathered Star points
8 rectangle F for Maple Leaf block stems
4 strips, each 4" x 43" from the lengthwise grain, for second border
32 triangle I for corner setting triangles
112 triangle N for third border

Note: Kazuko Wada cut identical triangles from the border print design and arranged them to form a kaleidoscopic effect.

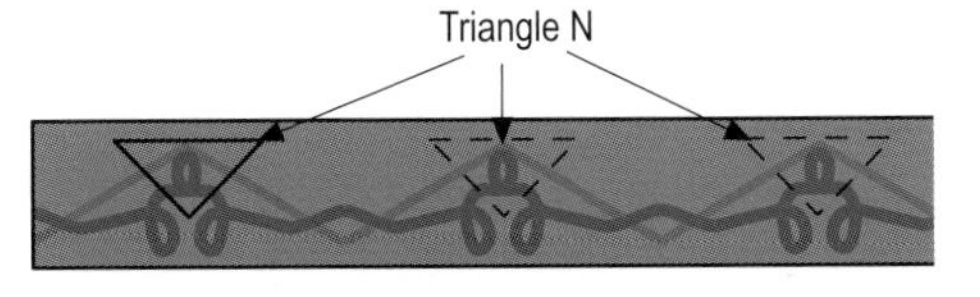

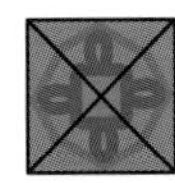

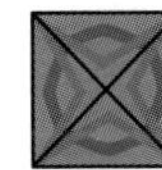

4 strips, each 4½" x 63", for fourth border
8 strips, each 1¼" x 16¼", for Feathered Star pieced corner units. Trim both ends of each strip at a 45° angle as shown to make a trapezoid.

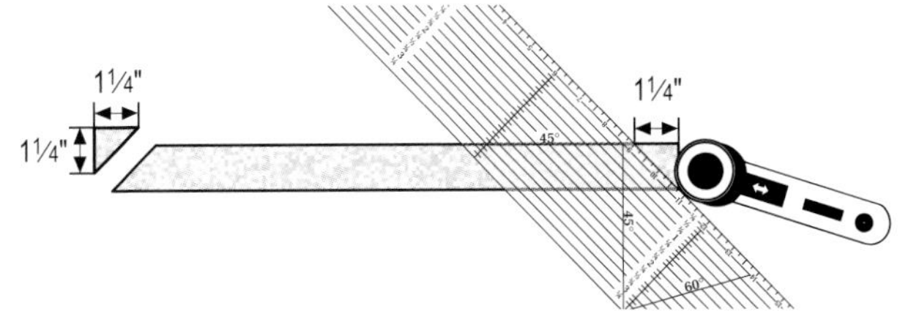

From beige print #1, cut:

4 triangle H for Feathered Star Medallion
4 *each* of piece G and G reversed for Feathered Star Medallion
32 triangle D for Maple Leaf blocks
16 square E for Maple Leaf blocks
8 triangle L for Feathered Star block (on pullout)
8 trapezoid J for Feathered Star block
4 each of piece K and K reversed for Feathered Star block
236 triangle N (124 for first border and 112 for third-border stars)
4 triangle O for first border
112 square P for third-border stars

From the blue print, cut:

48 triangle D for Feathered Star block
4 squares, each 1" x 1", for Feathered Star cornerstones
8 triangle I for Feathered Star block
8 triangle B for Feathered Star block
128 triangle O for third-border stars
6 strips, each 1½" x 42", for binding

From the assorted yellow prints, cut:

64 triangle D (32 for Feathered Star block and 32 for Maple Leaf blocks)
8 diamond C for Feathered Star block
24 square E for Maple Leaf blocks
36 square M for first border
96 triangle O for third-border stars

From the large-scale green-and-rust print, cut:

8 square E for Feathered Star block
28 square M for first border
60 triangle N for third border

From the small-scale rust print, cut:

8 triangle B for Feathered Star block

From the large-scale gold-and-blue print, cut:

4 strips, each 1" x 20½", for Feathered Star sashing strips
32 triangle S for third border
4 triangle T for third-border corners

From beige print #2, cut:

24 square Q for third border
4 triangle R for third border
76 triangle N for third border

Assembly

Feathered Star Center Block

1. Sew a rust print triangle B to 4 sides of the yellow border print octagon to make a square.

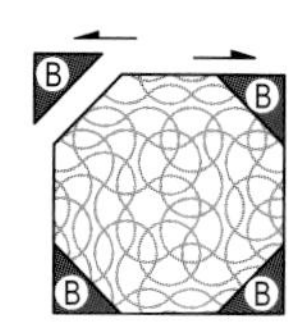

2. Sew a yellow print triangle D to a blue print triangle D.

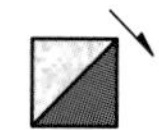

Half-Square Triangle Unit
Make 32.

3. Following the diagram below, arrange and sew 4 half-square triangle units and 2 blue print triangle D to make mirror-image pairs of feather units. Press the seam allowances toward the blue triangles.

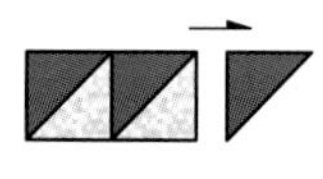

Make 8.

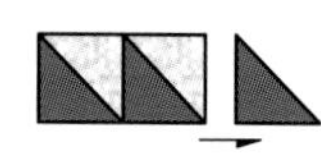

Make 8.

4. Arrange 2 mirror-image feather units made in step 3 with 1 each yellow border print kite A and A reversed, 1 rust triangle B, and 1 green-and-rust square E. Sew together in the order shown. Start or stop stitching ¼" from all seams that will be set in later.

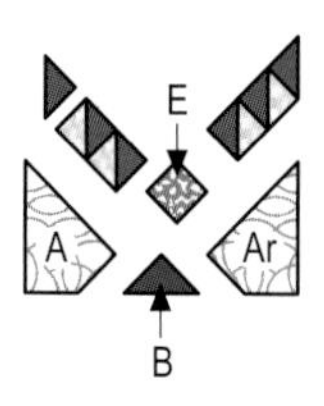

Make 4.

5. Fold under ¼" of the long edges of 1 yellow border print rectangle F to form the stem of the Maple Leaf block. Fold under each end ¼" and appliqué the stem diagonally to a beige #1 square E.

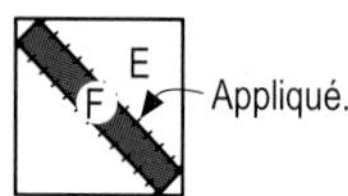

Make 8.

6. Sew a yellow print triangle D to a beige #1 triangle D to make a half-square triangle unit.

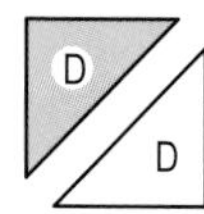

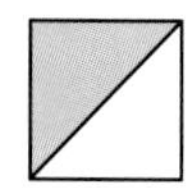

Make 32.

7. Arrange and join 1 beige #1 and 3 yellow print square E, 4 yellow-and-beige half-square triangle units, and 1 stem unit to make a Maple Leaf block. Make 8 blocks; set aside 4 for the third border.

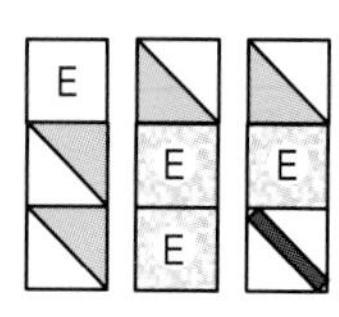

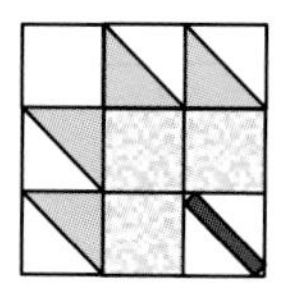

Maple Leaf Block
Make 8.

8. Add a yellow print diamond C to the end of each remaining feather unit made in step 3. Sew a green- and-rust square E to the end of 4 feather units as shown.

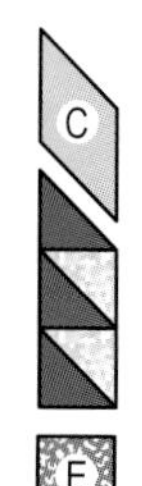

Make 4.

Make 4.

9. Sew a beige #1 piece G and a G reversed to adjacent sides of 4 Maple Leaf blocks as shown. Press the seam allowances toward the G pieces. Sew the corner seam last; press the seam open or to one side.

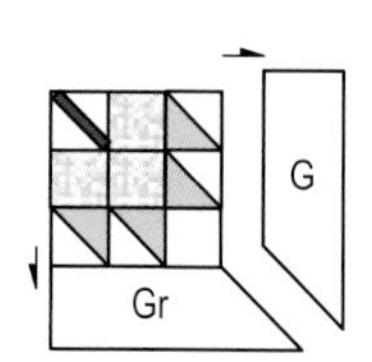

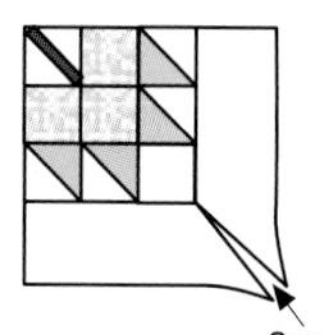

Sew last.

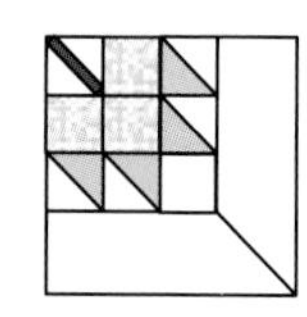

Make 4.

10. Following the diagram below, arrange and join the units made in steps 4, 8, and 9.

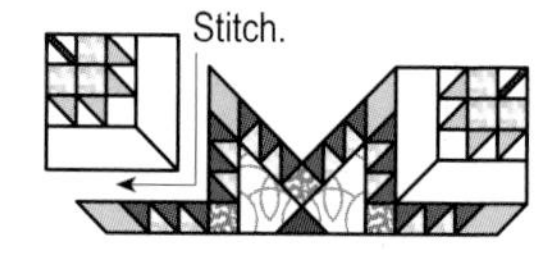

11. Sew a unit made in step 4 to opposite sides of the square made in step 1. Sew a unit made in step 10 to each side.

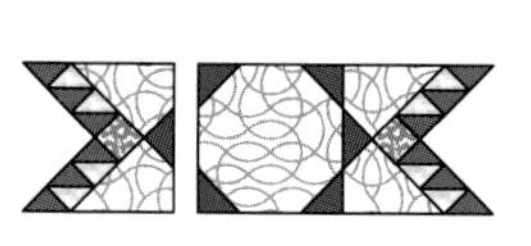

12. Set in each triangle H to make the Feathered Star block.

Feathered Star Block

13. Sew a 1" x 20½" gold-and-blue print strip to opposite sides of the Feathered Star block. Press the seams toward the strips. Add a 1" x 1" blue print cornerstone to each end of the 2 remaining gold-and-blue print strips, then sew to the top and bottom of the center block.

Pieced Corner Units

1. Arrange 4 yellow border print triangle I as shown to make a square. Carefully match the patterns so they form a kaleidoscopic design.

Make 8.

2. Sew a beige #1 trapezoid J to a blue triangle I; sew 1 each of beige #1 pieces K and K reversed to a blue triangle B in pairs. Referring to the diagram, sew the pieced triangles to the pieced squares made in step 1. Sew a beige #1 triangle L to each side. Sew a 1¼" x 16¼" yellow border print strip to 2 adjacent edges of the pieced corner unit. Miter the corners last.

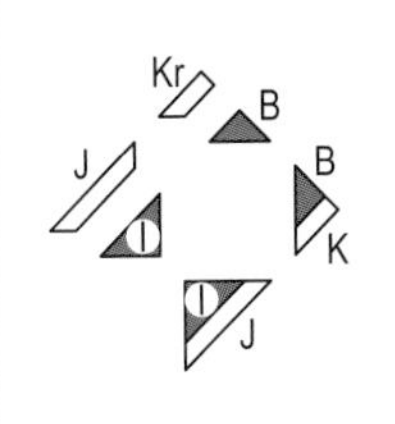

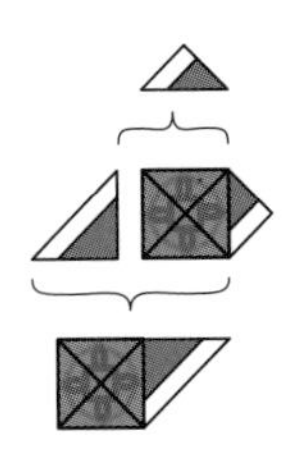
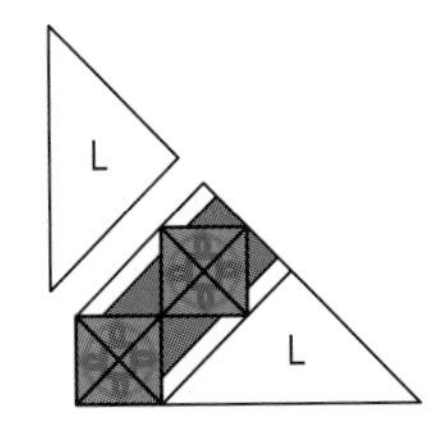

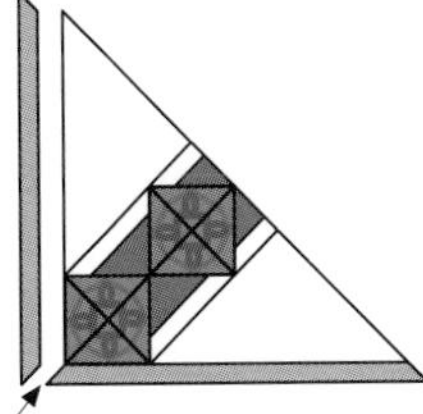
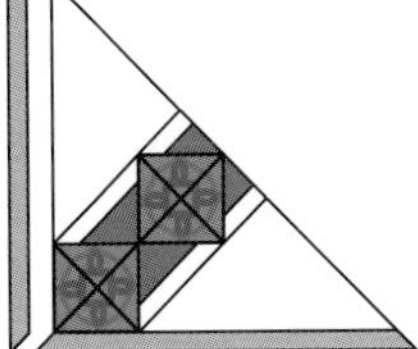
Sew last.

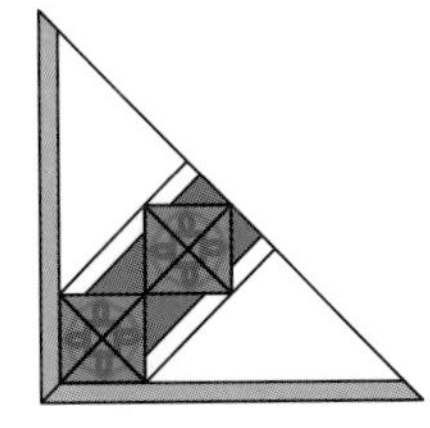
Pieced Corner Triangle
Make 4.

3. Sew a pieced corner unit to each side of the Feathered Star Medallion.

Feathered Star Medallion

First and Second Borders

1. Arrange and join 7 green-and-rust and 8 assorted yellow print square M with 28 beige #1 triangle N (for side borders) and 30 triangle N (for top and bottom borders). Place the darkest square at the border's center and gradate the values of the remaining squares, with the lightest yellow squares at the ends of the border. Add a beige #1 triangle N or O to each end of the border as shown.

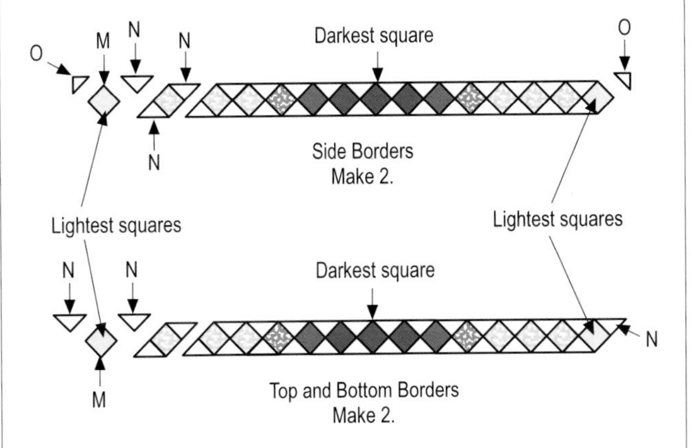

2. Arrange and join 1 yellow print square M, 2 beige #1 triangle N, and 1 beige #1 triangle O to make each corner unit.

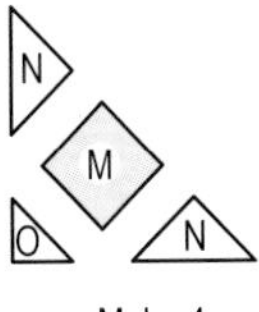

Make 4.

3. Sew the side border units to the sides of the quilt top, then add the top and bottom border units. Press the seams toward the center. Add the corner units last.

4. Sew the 4" x 43" yellow border print strips to the quilt top, mitering the corners.

Third and Fourth Borders

1. Arrange and join 1 beige #2 square Q, 2 beige #2 triangle N, and 2 green-and-rust triangle N to make each pieced triangle #1. Press the seam allowances toward the green-and-rust triangles.

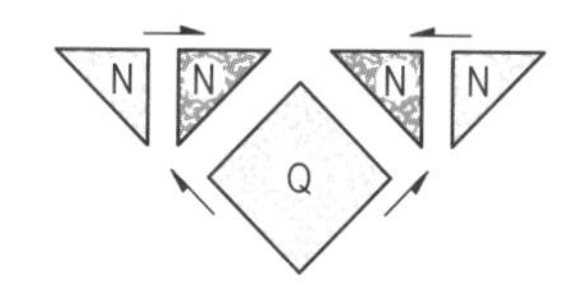

Pieced Triangle #1
Make 24.

2. Arrange and join 4 beige #1 square P, 4 beige #1 triangle N, 8 blue or 8 yellow print triangle O, and 4 yellow border print triangle N to make each Sawtooth Star block. Make 16 stars with blue points and 12 with assorted yellow points.

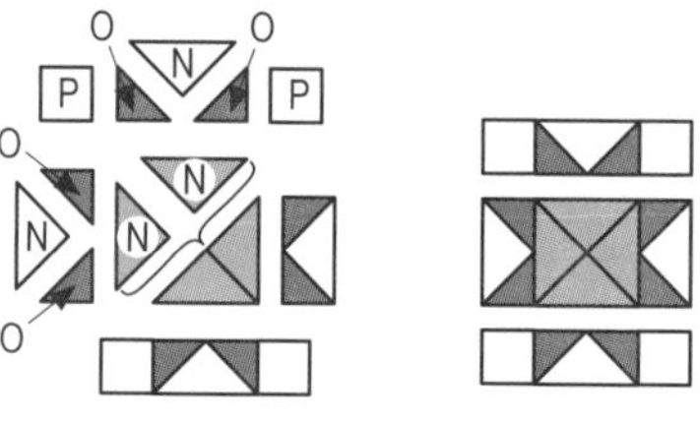

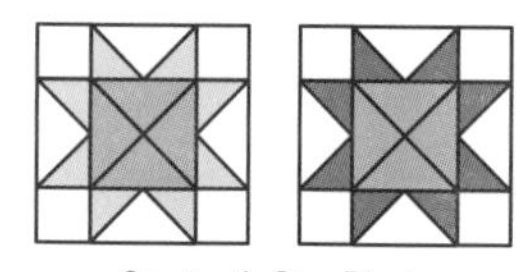

Sawtooth Star Blocks
Make 12 with yellow points.
Make 16 with blue points.

3. Arrange and join 3 beige #2 triangle N and 1 green-and-rust triangle N to make each pieced triangle #2.

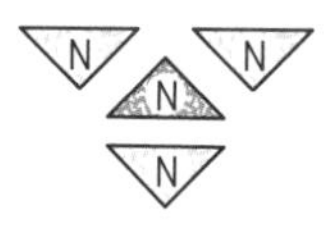

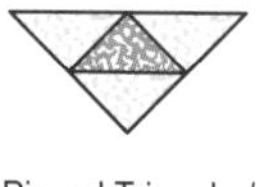

Pieced Triangle #2
Make 4.

4. Arrange and join 4 beige #2 triangle N, 1 beige #2 triangle R, and 2 green-and-rust triangle N to make each pieced triangle #3.

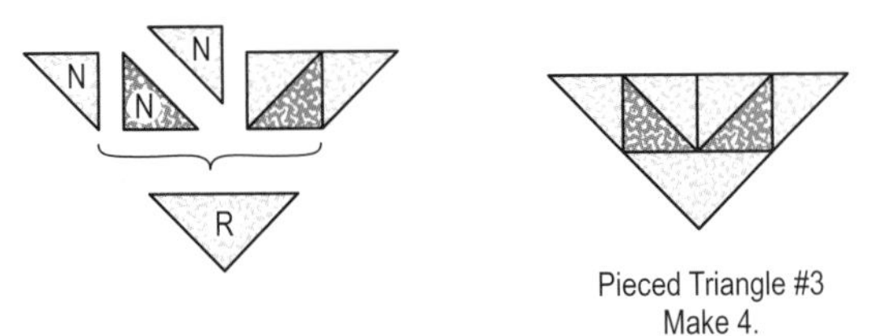

Pieced Triangle #3
Make 4.

5. Arrange and join 4 blue and 2 yellow Sawtooth Star blocks, 1 Maple Leaf block, 6 pieced triangle #1, 2 pieced triangle #2, and 6 gold-and-blue triangle S to make each of the side borders.

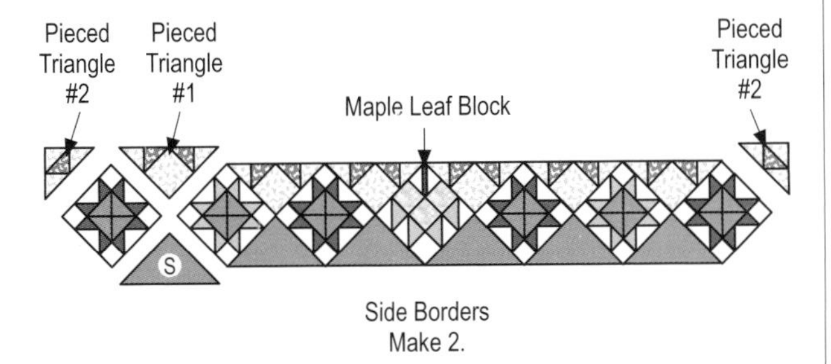

Side Borders
Make 2.

6. Arrange and join 4 blue and 2 yellow Sawtooth Star blocks, 1 Maple Leaf block, 6 pieced triangle #1, 2 pieced triangle #3, and 6 gold-and-blue triangle S to make each of the top and bottom borders.

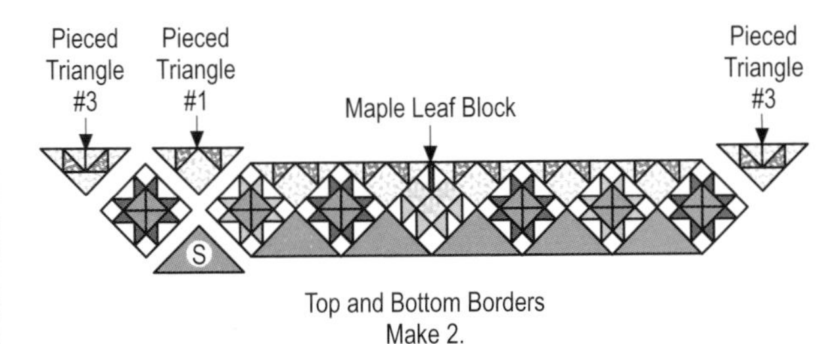

Top and Bottom Borders
Make 2.

7. Arrange and join 1 yellow Sawtooth Star block, 2 gold-and-blue triangle S, and 1 gold-and-blue triangle T to make each pieced corner unit.

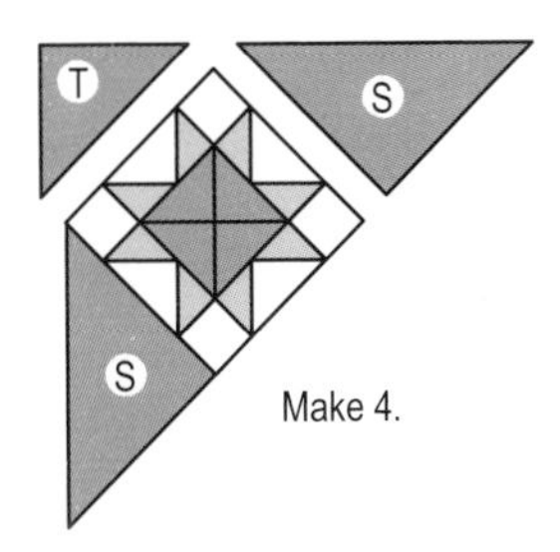

Make 4.

8. Add the side borders to opposite sides of the quilt top, then add the top and bottom borders. Press the seams toward the border. Add the pieced corner units last, matching the seams.

9. Stitch the 4½" x 63" yellow border print strips to the quilt top; miter the corners, matching the stripe.

Finishing

1. Layer the quilt top with backing and batting; baste.
2. Quilt as desired.
3. Bind the edges.

straight of grain

A
Kinkakuji
Cut 8 yellow border print

D
Kinkakuji

¼" seam allowance

E
Kinkakuji
Cut 16 beige print #1
Cut 24 assorted yellow prints
Cut 8 green-and-rust print

Cut 32 beige print #1
Cut 48 blue print
Cut 64 assorted yellow prints

C
Kinkakuji
Cut 8 assorted yellow prints

G
Kinkakuji
Cut 4 and 4r beige print #1

H
Kinkakuji
Cut 4 beige print #1

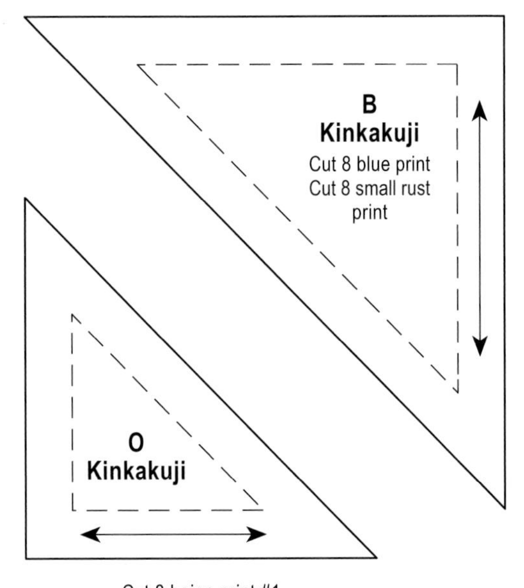

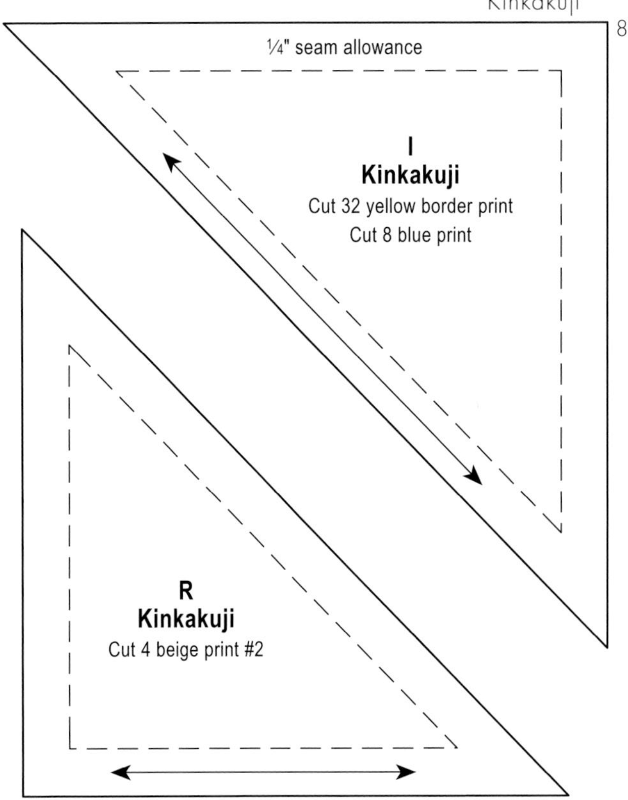

Note: Template L is on the pullout.

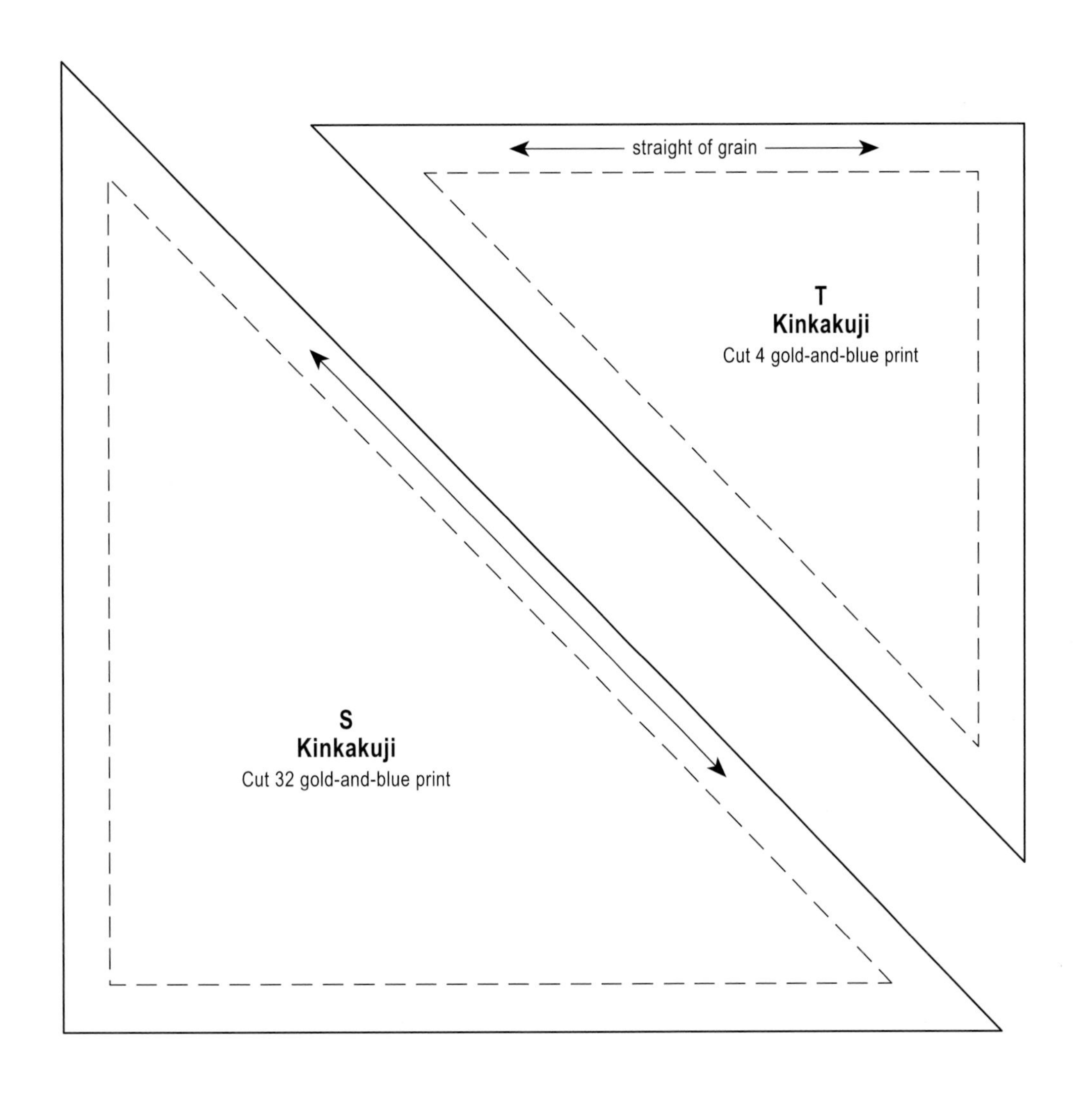

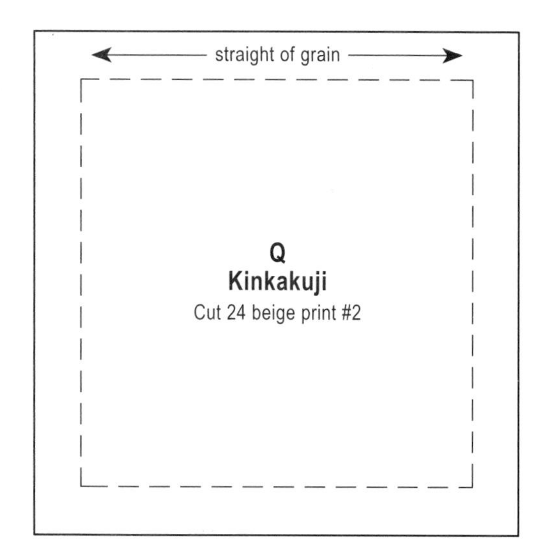
straight of grain
Q
Kinkakuji
Cut 24 beige print #2

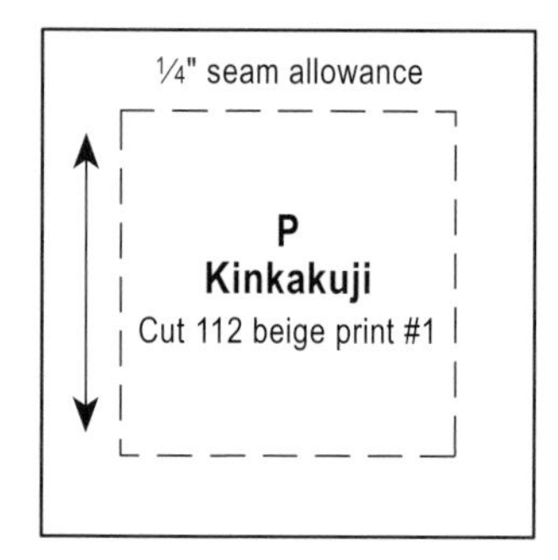
¼" seam allowance
P
Kinkakuji
Cut 112 beige print #1

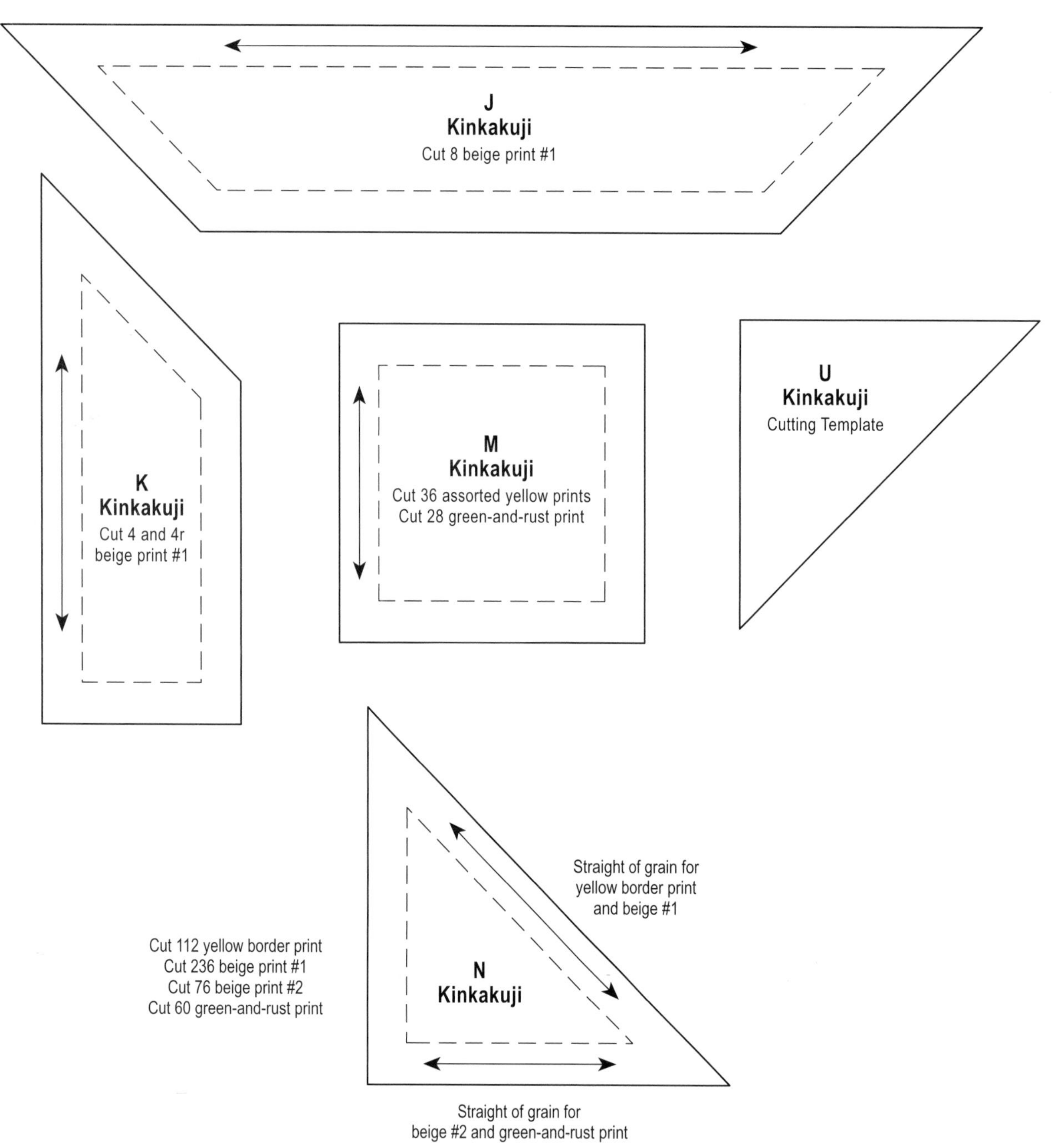
F
Kinkakuji
Cut 8 yellow border print
Add seam allowance for appliqué piece.
J
Kinkakuji
Cut 8 beige print #1
K
Kinkakuji
Cut 4 and 4r
beige print #1
M
Kinkakuji
Cut 36 assorted yellow prints
Cut 28 green-and-rust print
U
Kinkakuji
Cutting Template
Straight of grain for
yellow border print
and beige #1
Cut 112 yellow border print
Cut 236 beige print #1
Cut 76 beige print #2
Cut 60 green-and-rust print
N
Kinkakuji
Straight of grain for
beige #2 and green-and-rust print

Hatsu Haru *(New Year's Day)*

Finished quilt size: 26½" x 32¾"
Finished block size: 5½" x 5½"

In Japan, New Year's is celebrated with as much fervor as Christmas in the West. We think of January as the beginning of a new year, so on December 31, we clean the house thoroughly inside and out. However, we do not clean or sew on January 1 because it is believed that if we do, we will have to clean and sew continuously all year.

Similar to the western custom of putting Christmas wreaths on doors, people in Japan hang a shi-me kazari, *a Japanese wreath. It is made from rope, pine branches, and a variety of materials, each having a symbolic meaning. We also set flower pots (called* kadomatsu*) containing bamboo and pine branches outside on both sides of the doorway in preparation for the new year.*

Many phrases pertaining to New Year's customs begin with hatsu, *or "first," emphasizing things done for the first time that year. The sunrise on January 1 is called* hatsu-hinode, *or "first sunrise," and many people rise very early to view this special moment and to pray. The first dream of the new year is called* hatsu-yume *and is believed to have a significant meaning. The first trip to a temple is called* hatsu-mode.

When the year changes, we leave all the unpleasant events behind and look forward to a new year full of hope and aspiration.

Materials: 44"-wide fabric

Note: I used silk *kimono* fabrics for this quilt.

½ yd. cotton muslin for block foundations
Assorted scraps (at least 6" x 6" each) of 19 multicolored prints for Crazy piecing
⅛ yd. or 8" x 8" scrap of yellow solid for block centers
Assorted scraps (at least 6" x 6" each) of 14 solids for Crazy piecing
¼ yd. light blue solid for sashing
½ yd. OR 20" x 30" rectangle of purple print for borders
¼ yd. lavender print for binding
1 yd. for backing
12 assorted embellishments, such as brass charms, ribbon roses, and cord knots, for block centers
30" x 37" piece of batting

Cutting

Cut all strips across the width of the fabric from selvage to selvage unless otherwise noted. Use the template on page 90.

From the muslin, cut:
12 squares, each 6" x 6"
From the yellow solid, cut:
12 piece #1 for block centers
From the light blue solid, cut:
9 strips, each 1¼" x 6", for sashing
2 strips, each 1¼" x 24¾", for sashing
2 strips, each 1¼" x 22½", for inner border
2 strips, each 1¼" x 30½", for inner border
From the purple print, cut:
2 strips, each 3¾" x 27½", for outer border
2 strips, each 3¾" x 28", for outer border
From the backing fabric, cut:
1 rectangle, 30" x 37"
From the lavender print, cut:
4 strips, each 1" wide, for binding

Assembly

Note: There are no templates for the strips surrounding piece #1. Cut strips or scraps of fabric as you need them to sew to the blocks. Cutting the scraps roughly rectangular, with a wide and a narrow end, adds to the Crazy effect. Vary the widths of the strips, using narrower strips (½" to ¾" finished) for the center section of the block and cutting them wider (1½" to 2" finished) as you progress to the outer edges.

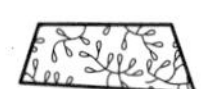

1. Pin a yellow piece #1 to the center of each muslin square. Rotate the placement of each piece #1 from square to square to resemble a variety of rose blossoms.

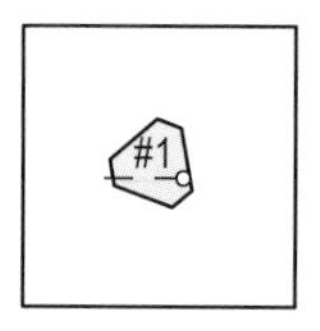

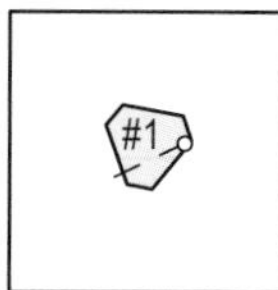

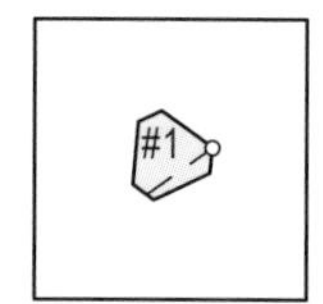

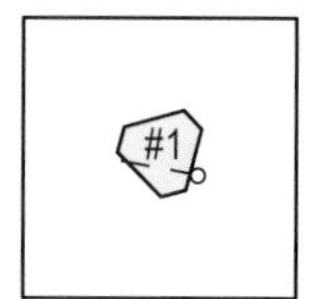

2. For piece #2, cut a scrap of fabric approximately 1" x 2". Place piece #2 on top of one long side of piece #1, right sides together and raw edges even. Stitch through all 3 layers. Flip piece #2 to the right side and press.

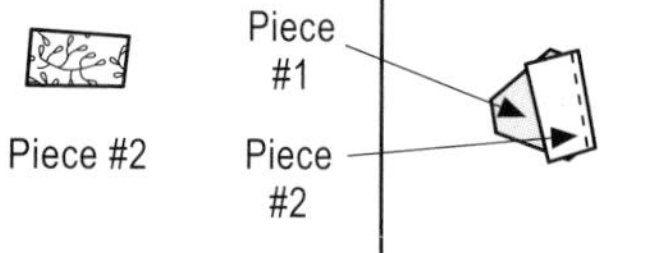

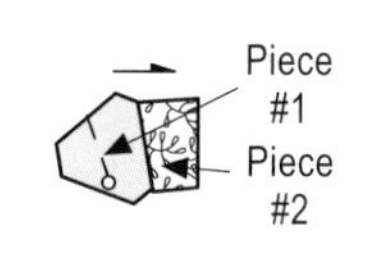

3. For pieces #3 and #4, cut strips approximately the same size as you did for piece #2. Sew a piece to each remaining long side of piece #1. Flip pieces #3 and #4 to the right side and press.

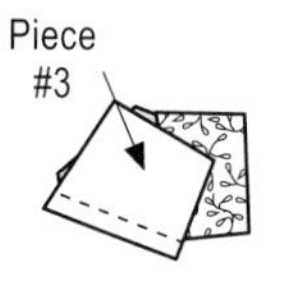

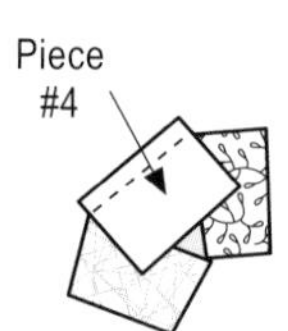

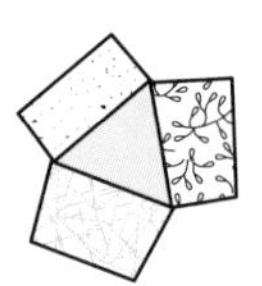

4. Draw a straight line across the ends of each pair of strips, drawing at random angles to create a Crazy piecing sequence. With scissors, trim the ends along the drawn lines, being careful not to cut the muslin.

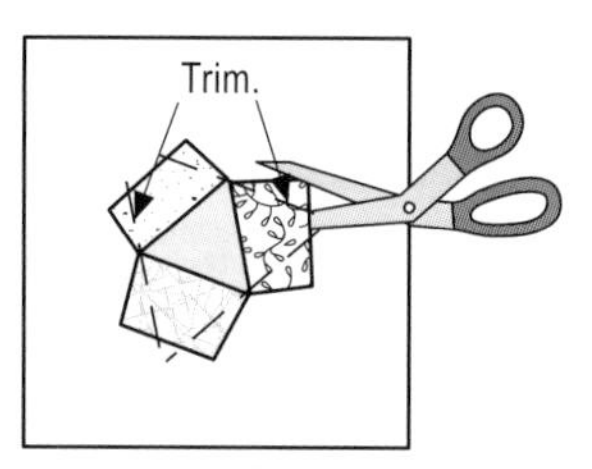

5. Cut 3 more strips long enough to reach from edge to edge of the previously pieced strips. With right sides together and raw edges even, sew each new strip to the unit made in steps 2 and 3. Repeat step 4.

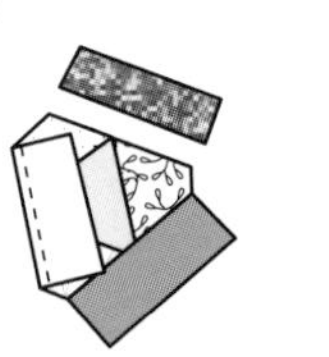

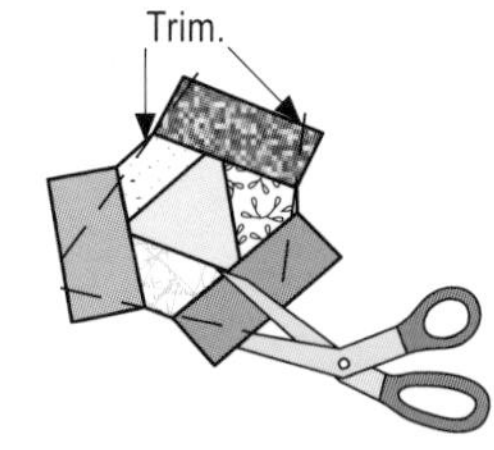

Note: Piece #1 has now become a hexagon, with 3 long sides and 3 short sides.

6. Continue cutting, sewing, and trimming strips in groups of 3, cutting wider and more uneven rectangles as you approach the outer edges of the muslin foundation. Sew about the same number of pieces to each foundation.

Note: Remember, when sewing a strip to the foundation, always sew it to 3 different pieces. When you reach the corners, you may need to sew the scrap to only 1 or 2 pieces.

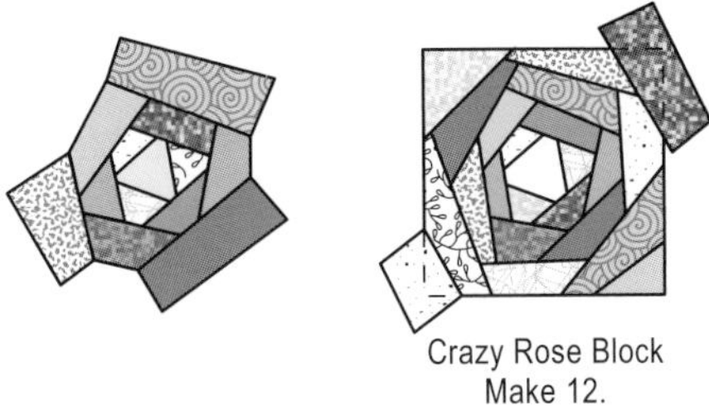

Crazy Rose Block
Make 12.

7. After covering the muslin foundation with strips, turn the block over and trim it to measure 6" x 6".

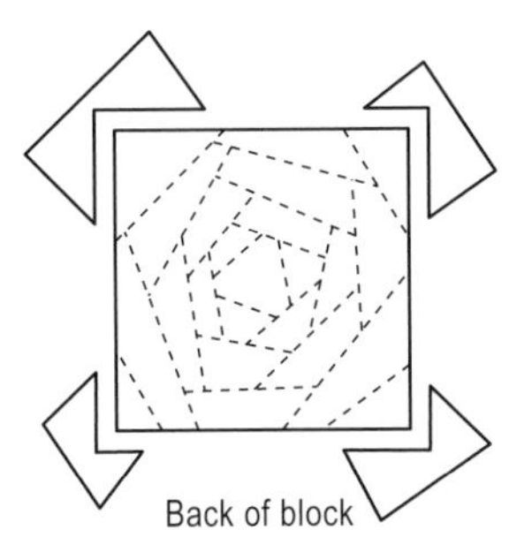

Back of block

8. Arrange the blocks in 3 vertical rows of 4 blocks each. Sew a 1¼" x 6" light blue horizontal sashing strip between the blocks as shown. Sew a 1¼" x 24¾" light blue vertical sashing strip between each row. Press the seams toward the sashing strips.

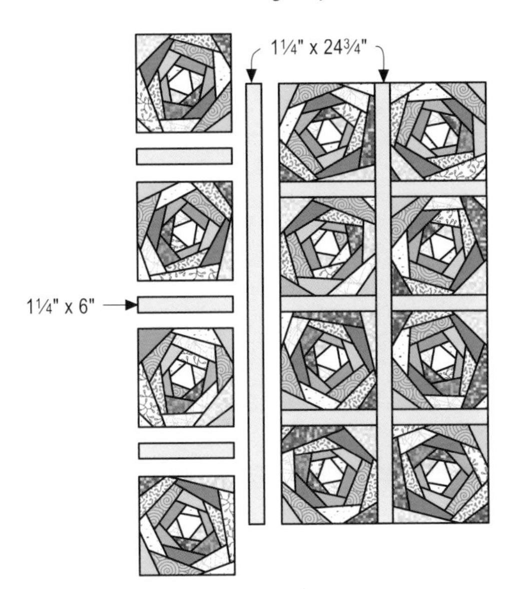

Borders

1. Sew the 1¼" x 30½" light blue side inner borders and the 1¼" x 22½" top and bottom inner borders to the quilt top. Press the seams toward the borders. Miter the corners; press the seam allowances open and trim to ¼".

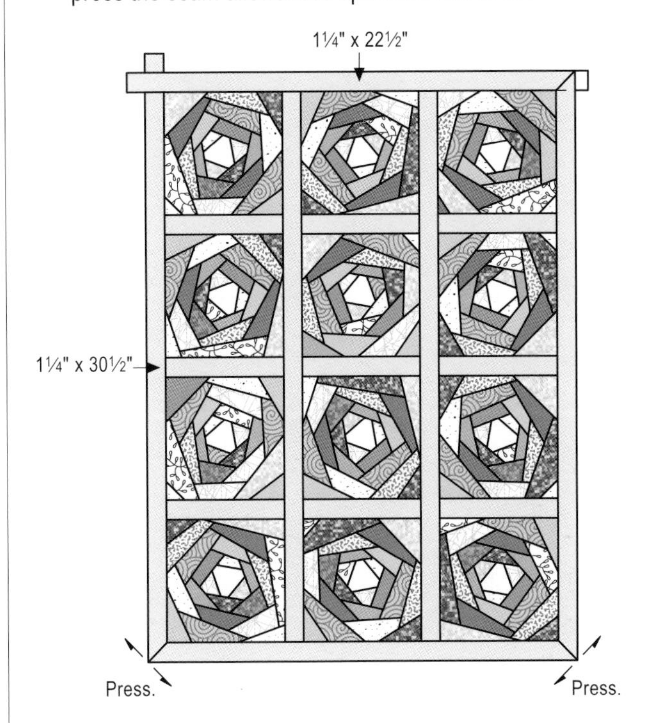

2. Measure the quilt through the center from top to bottom. Trim each 3¾" x 27½" purple print outer border strip to this measurement and sew to the sides of the quilt top.

3. Measure the quilt through the center from side to side, including the borders just added. Trim each 3¾" x 28"

purple print strip to this measurement and sew to the top and bottom of the quilt top.

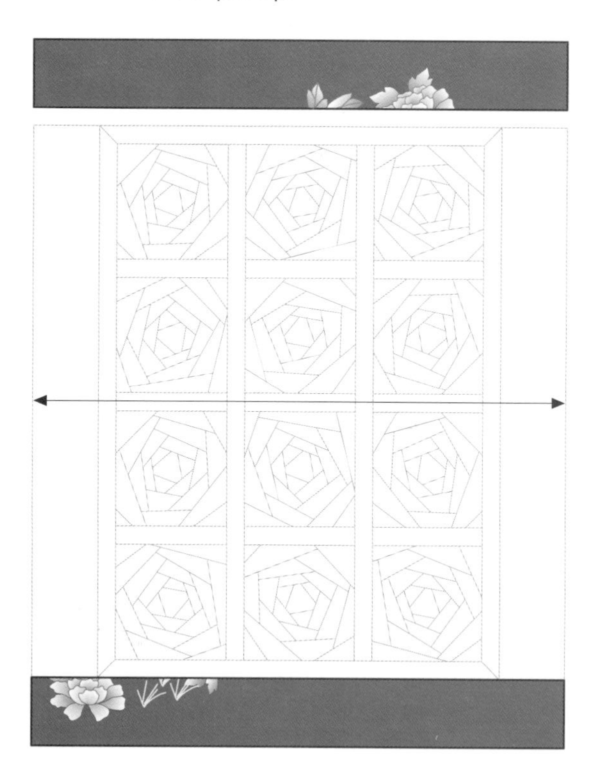

Finishing

1. Layer the quilt top with batting and backing; baste.
2. Quilt in-the-ditch along the sashing and inner borders or as desired. Quilt the outer borders, following the print design of the fabric.
3. Bind the edges.
4. Attach embellishments to the center of each Crazy block.

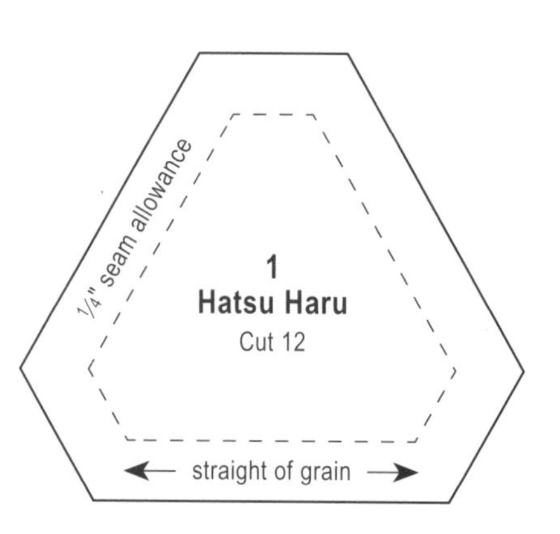

Kamon *(Family Crest)*

Finished quilt size: 11" x 11"

It is said this simple, yet beautiful symbol was first used in the eleventh century. The members of noble society, such as the samurai, *used these symbols as a type of logo on flags and armour to represent their power and to differentiate sides in battle during that age of civil wars. When those tumultuous times passed, the* kamon *was used as a symbol on furniture and clothing to represent the nobility of the family.*

In the peaceful Edo period, culture developed rapidly, and art forms such as ukiyoe *woodblock prints and* kabuki *plays became popular. The* kamon *became a logo used by many artists, and new designs developed as these symbols became more and more fashionable.* Kamon *designs consist of geometric shapes, animals, or objects found in nature, such as birds, plants, mountains, and other interesting shapes. Today, the* kamon *is seen only occasionally on women's* kimono, *and many young people are unaware of their family's* kamon.

Materials: 44"-wide fabric

Note: I used silk *kimono* fabrics for the appliqués.

3" x 10" rectangle of purple print for flowers
5" x 5" square *each* of green, blue, and pink prints for leaves
11½" x 11½" square of white-on-white print for appliqué background (Template #6)
5" x 44" strip of gray-and-metallic print for checkerboard
3" x 44" strip of beige print for checkerboard
12" to 18" *each* of purple, pink, blue, and green embroidery floss
2 squares, *each* 10¾" x 10¾", for backing
12" x 12" piece of batting
Extra batting for stuffing flowers and leaves
2 squares, each 9¾" x 9¾", of poster-weight cardboard

Cutting

Cut all strips across the width of the fabric from selvage to selvage unless otherwise noted. Use the templates on page 95.

Note: I recommend using freezer-paper appliqué for "Kamon."

From the green print, cut:
1 each of leaf #1 and #1 reversed

From the blue print, cut:
1 each of leaf #2 and #2 reversed

From the pink print, cut:
1 leaf #3

From the purple print, cut:
1 flower #4
2 flowers #5

From the gray-and-metallic print, cut:
3 strips, each 1½" wide. From 1 of the strips, cut 24 squares, each 1½" x 1½", for checkerboard. From the remaining 2 strips, cut 4 strips, each 1½" x 11½", for binding.

From the beige print, cut:
1 strip, 1½" wide; cut into 24 squares, each 1½" x 1½", for checkerboard

From 1 of the cardboard squares, cut:
1 circle, 9½" in diameter

Assembly

1. Trace and cut out the freezer-paper patterns. Place the shiny side of the paper down on the *wrong* side of the appliqué fabric; press with a dry iron (no steam) for about 3 seconds to adhere the freezer paper to the fabric.

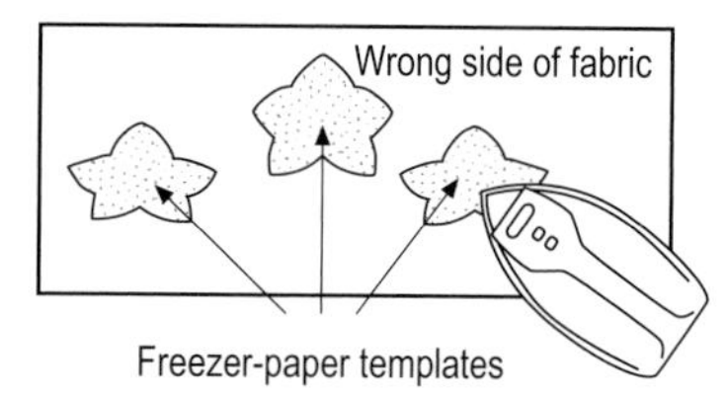

2. Cut out each appliqué piece, adding ¼"-wide seam allowances around each freezer-paper pattern. If desired, fold the seam allowances over the edge of the paper and baste. Clip inside corners as necessary.

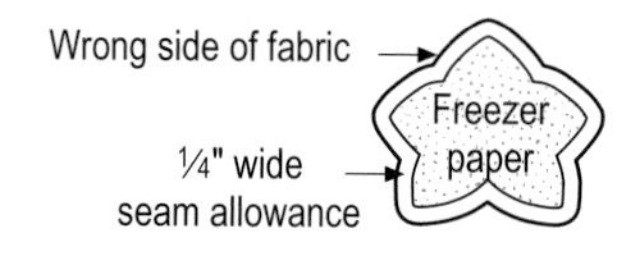

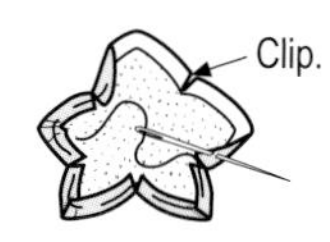

3. Using the placement diagram on page 95, transfer the appliqué design only to the 11½" white-on-white background square, centering the circle.
4. Position and appliqué leaves #1 and #2, and #1 and #2 reversed in numerical order, leaving an opening where the next leaf will overlap. If you did not baste the edges first, turn under the seam allowance, using the edge of the freezer paper as a guide. Remove the basting and gently remove the freezer paper through the opening. Insert a small amount of batting into each leaf to puff it up a little before appliquéing the next leaf. Spread the batting evenly.

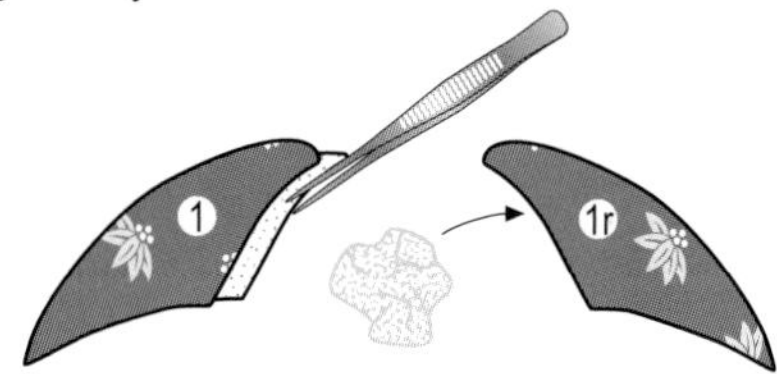

Remove freezer paper, then stuff.

5. Appliqué leaf #3 and flowers #4 and #5 in numerical order, leaving a small opening along a straight edge. Remove the freezer paper and basting; stuff the piece, then finish the appliqué.

6. On a sheet of typing paper, trace and cut out the half-circle pattern on page 95. Fold the appliquéd fabric in half vertically. Align the dotted center line of the half-circle pattern with the fold of the fabric; pin, then cut out the appliqué circle, adding a ¼"-wide seam allowance.

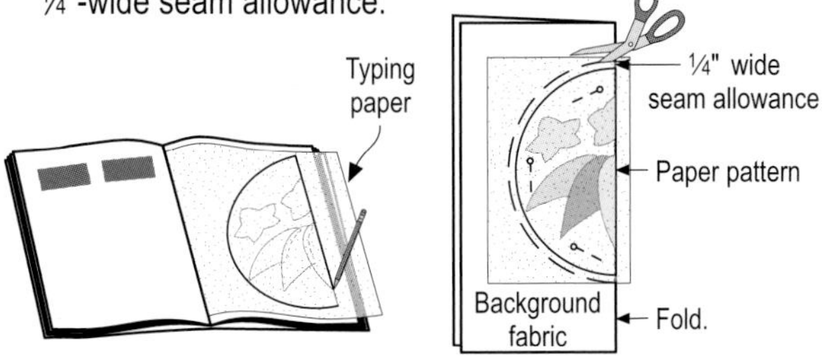

7. Sew the gray-and-metallic and beige squares together to make a checkerboard background.

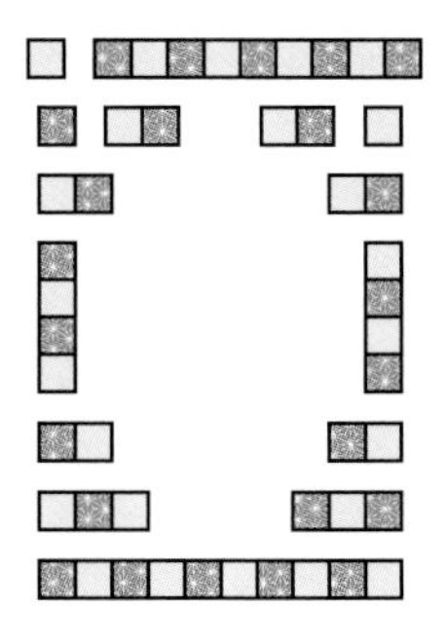

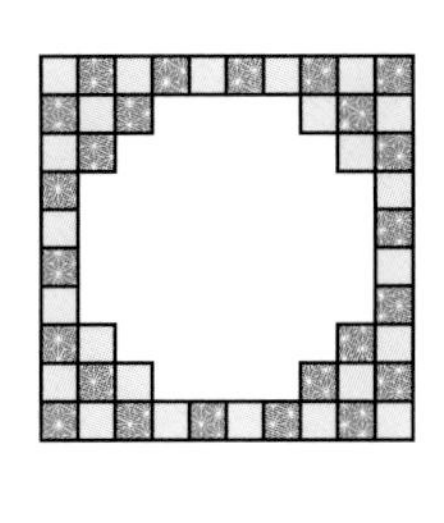

8. Hand baste a row of running stitches ⅛" from the edge of the appliqué circle.

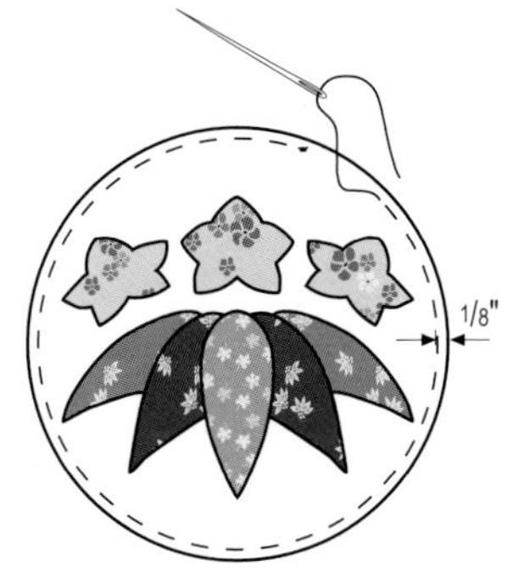

9. Center the cardboard circle on the back side of the appliqué circle and gently pull the basting thread, bringing the seam allowance over the cardboard circle. When you have a smooth, centered appliqué circle, press the seam allowances, forming a crease. Remove the cardboard.

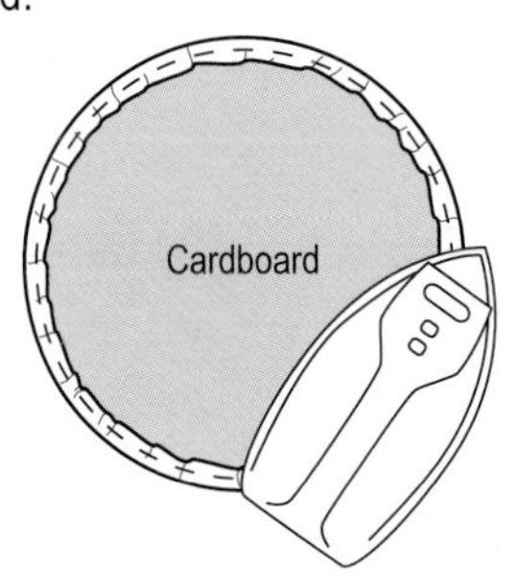

10. Center and pin the appliqué circle on top of the checkerboard background; appliqué in place.

Finishing

1. Layer the quilt top with batting only; baste.
2. Quilt the appliqué circle, following the design of the background fabric or as desired. Quilt the appliqué and checkerboard pieces in-the-ditch. Embroider the details of the leaves and flowers, using a stem or outline stitch and matching the color of the thread to each piece. Refer to the placement diagram on page 95.
3. Trim excess batting.
4. Sew a 1½" x 11½" gray-and-metallic binding strip to the sides of the quilt top. Trim the ends. Sew the top and bottom binding strips to the quilt top.

5. Layer the 10¾" backing squares on the back of the quilt, right side out. Turn the edges of the binding to the back to make a ½"-wide binding on 3 sides, leaving the top edge unbound.

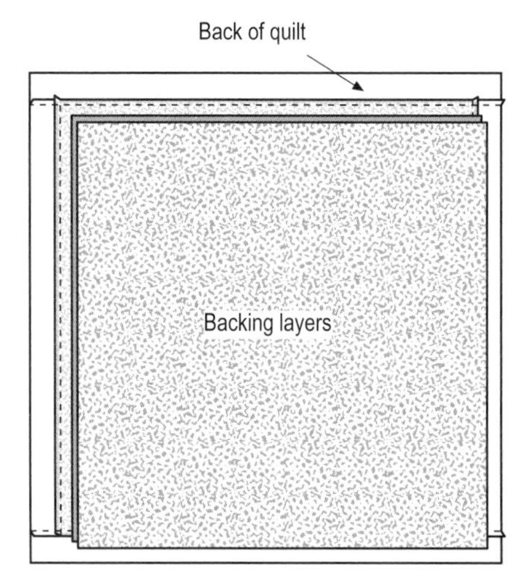

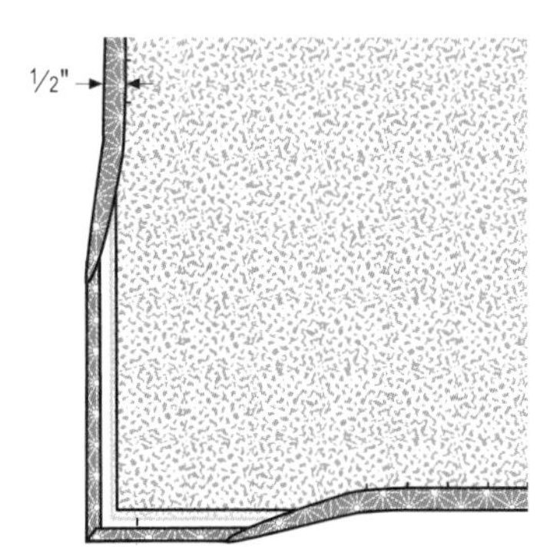

6. Insert the remaining 9¾" cardboard square between the backing layers and bind the remaining edge.

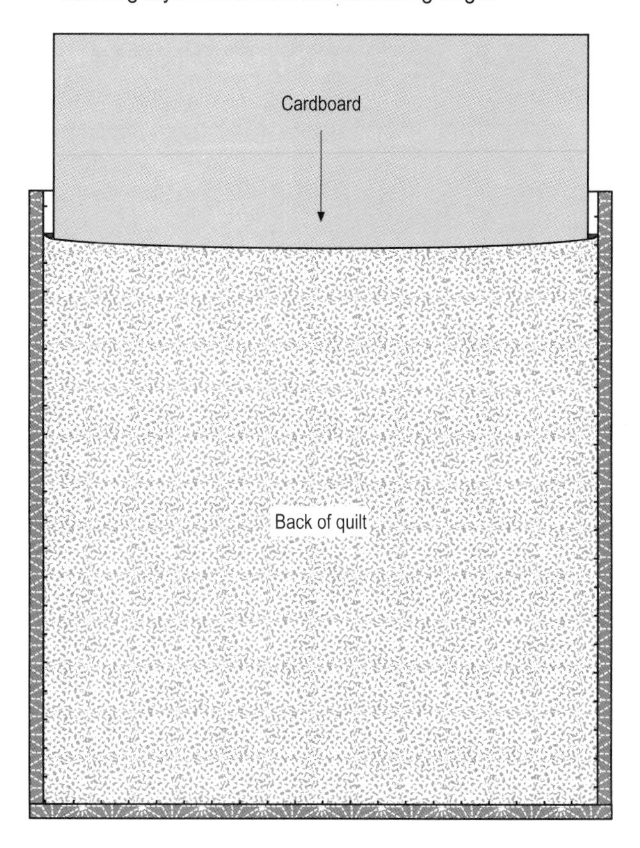

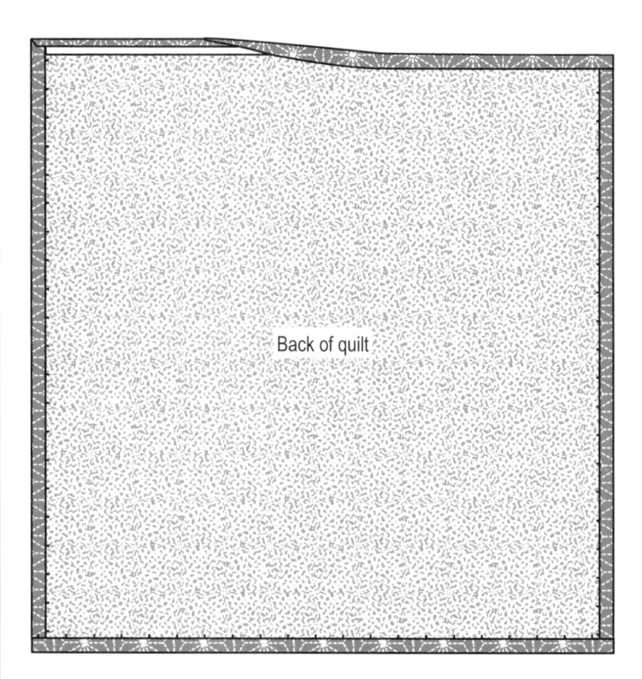

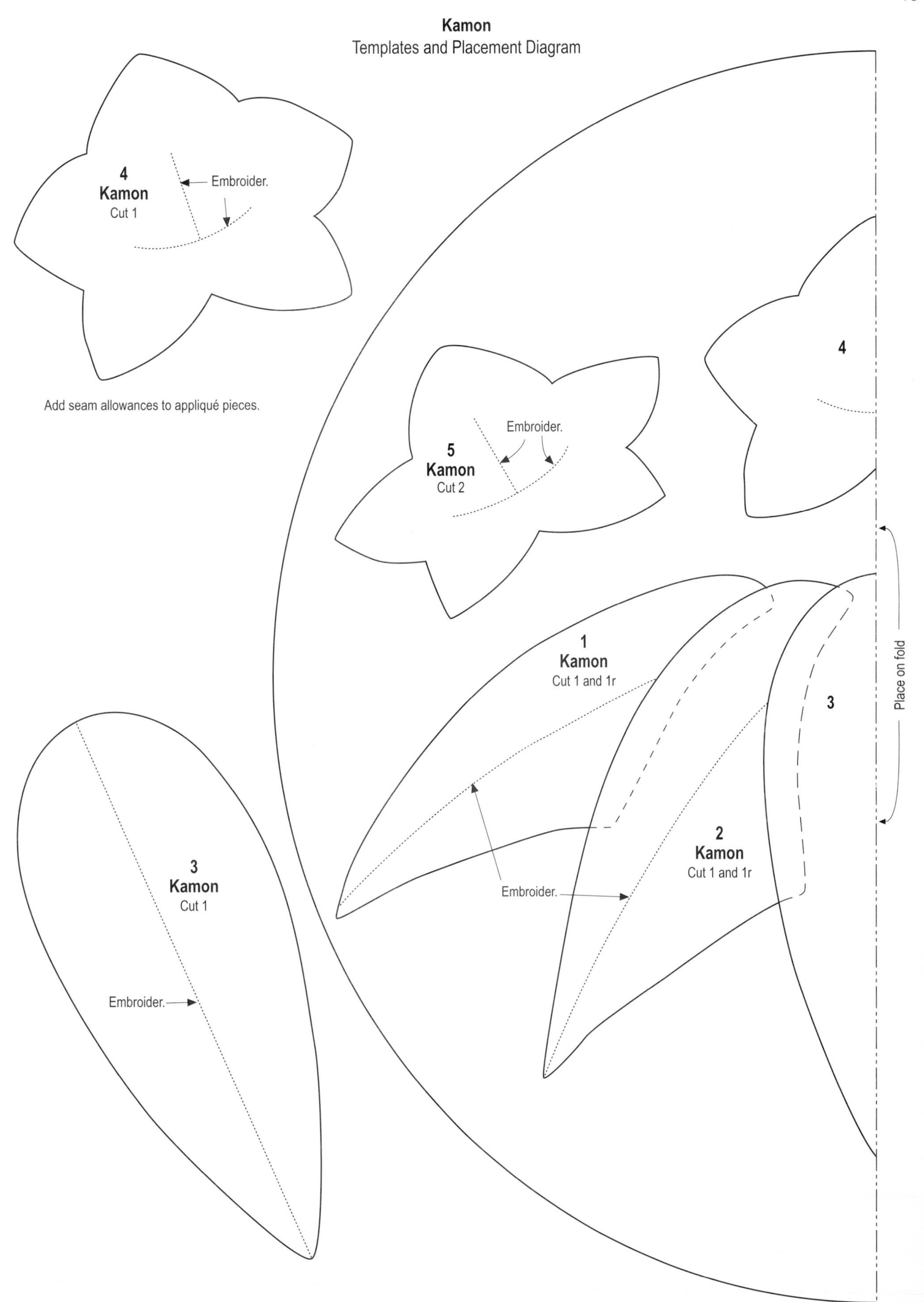
Kamon
Templates and Placement Diagram
4
Kamon
Cut 1
Embroider.
Add seam allowances to appliqué pieces.
5
Kamon
Cut 2
Embroider.
4
1
Kamon
Cut 1 and 1r
Place on fold
3
2
Kamon
Cut 1 and 1r
Embroider.
3
Kamon
Cut 1
Embroider.

Publications and Products

THAT PATCHWORK PLACE TITLES:

AMERICA'S BEST-LOVED QUILT BOOKS®

All the Blocks Are Geese • Mary Sue Suit
All New Copy Art for Quilters
All-Star Sampler • Roxanne Carter
Angle Antics • Mary Hickey
Appliqué in Bloom • Gabrielle Swain
Appliquilt® • Tonee White
Appliquilt® for Christmas • Tonee White
Appliquilt® Your ABCs • Tonee White
Around the Block with Judy Hopkins
At Home with Quilts • Nancy J. Martin
Baltimore Bouquets • Mimi Dietrich
Bargello Quilts • Marge Edie
Bias Square® Miniatures • Christine Carlson
Biblical Blocks • Rosemary Makhan
Blockbender Quilts • Margaret J. Miller
Block by Block • Beth Donaldson
Borders by Design • Paulette Peters
Calicoes & Quilts Unlimited • Judy Betts Morrison
The Cat's Meow • Janet Kime
Celebrate! with Little Quilts • Alice Berg, Sylvia Johnson & Mary Ellen Von Holt
Celebrating the Quilt
Class-Act Quilts
Classic Quilts with Precise Foundation Piecing • Tricia Lund & Judy Pollard
Colourwash Quilts • Deirdre Amsden
Country Medallion Sampler • Carol Doak
Crazy Rags • Deborah Brunner
Decorate with Quilts & Collections • Nancy J. Martin
Down the Rotary Road with Judy Hopkins
The Easy Art of Appliqué • Mimi Dietrich & Roxi Eppler
Easy Machine Paper Piecing • Carol Doak
Easy Mix & Match Machine Paper Piecing • Carol Doak
Easy Paper-Pieced Keepsake Quilts • Carol Doak
Easy Reversible Vests • Carol Doak
A Fine Finish • Cody Mazuran
Five- and Seven-Patch Blocks & Quilts for the ScrapSaver • Judy Hopkins
Four-Patch Blocks & Quilts for the ScrapSaver • Judy Hopkins
Freedom in Design • Mia Rozmyn
From a Quilter's Garden • Gabrielle Swain
Go Wild with Quilts • Margaret Rolfe
Go Wild with Quilts—Again! • Margaret Rolfe
Great Expectations • Karey Bresenhan with Alice Kish & Gay E. McFarland
Hand-Dyed Fabric Made Easy • Adriene Buffington
Happy Endings • Mimi Dietrich
Honoring the Seasons • Takako Onoyama
Jacket Jazz • Judy Murrah
Jacket Jazz Encore • Judy Murrah
The Joy of Quilting • Joan Hanson & Mary Hickey
Little Quilts • Alice Berg, Sylvia Johnson & Mary Ellen Von Holt
Lively Little Logs • Donna McConnell
Loving Stitches • Jeana Kimball
Machine Quilting Made Easy • Maurine Noble
Magic Base Blocks for Unlimited Quilt Designs • Patty Barney & Cooky Schock
Mirror Manipulations • Gail Valentine
More Jazz from Judy Murrah
Nine-Patch Blocks & Quilts for the ScrapSaver • Judy Hopkins
Patchwork Pantry • Suzette Halferty & Carol C. Porter
A Perfect Match • Donna Lynn Thomas
A Pioneer Doll and Her Quilts • Mary Hickey
Prairie People—Cloth Dolls to Make and Cherish • Marji Hadley & J. Dianne Ridgley
Press for Success • Myrna Giesbrecht
Quilted for Christmas, Book II
Quilted for Christmas, Book III
Quilted Landscapes • Joan Blalock
Quilted Legends of the West • Judy Zehner & Kim Mosher
Quilted Sea Tapestries • Ginny Eckley
Quilting Design Sourcebook • Dorothy Osler
Quilting Makes the Quilt • Lee Cleland
Quilting Up a Storm • Lydia Quigley
Quilts: An American Legacy • Mimi Dietrich
Quilts for Baby • Ursula Reikes
Quilts for Red-Letter Days • Janet Kime
Quilts from the Smithsonian • Mimi Dietrich
Refrigerator Art Quilts • Jennifer Paulson
Repiecing the Past • Sara Rhodes Dillow
Rotary Riot • Judy Hopkins & Nancy J. Martin
Rotary Roundup • Judy Hopkins & Nancy J. Martin
Round Robin Quilts • Pat Magaret & Donna Slusser
Seasoned with Quilts • Retta Warehime
Sensational Settings • Joan Hanson
Shortcuts: A Concise Guide to Rotary Cutting • Donna Lynn Thomas
Simply Scrappy Quilts • Nancy J. Martin
Small Talk • Donna Lynn Thomas
Square Dance • Martha Thompson
Start with Squares • Martha Thompson
Strip-Pieced Watercolor Magic • Deanna Spingola
Stripples • Donna Lynn Thomas
Sunbonnet Sue All Through the Year • Sue Linker
Template-Free® Quiltmaking • Trudie Hughes
Template-Free® Quilts and Borders • Trudie Hughes
Through the Window & Beyond • Lynne Edwards
Traditional Blocks Meet Appliqué • Deborah J. Moffett-Hall
Victorian Elegance • Lezette Thomason
Watercolor Impressions • Pat Magaret & Donna Slusser
Watercolor Quilts • Pat Magaret & Donna Slusser
Watercolor Quilts 1997 Calendar • Pat Magaret & Donna Slusser
Weave It! Quilt It! Wear It! • Mary Anne Caplinger
Woven & Quilted • Mary Anne Caplinger
WOW! Wool-on-Wool Folk Art Quilts • Janet Carija Brandt

4", 6", 8" & metric Bias Square® • BiRangle™
Ruby Beholder® • ScrapMaster • Rotary Rule™
Rotary Mate™ • Bias Stripper®
Shortcuts to America's Best-Loved Quilts (video)

FIBER STUDIO PRESS TITLES:

Complex Cloth • Jane Dunnewold
Erika Carter: Personal Imagery in Art Quilts • Erika Carter
Inspiration Odyssey • Diana Swim Wessel
The Nature of Design • Joan Colvin
Velda Newman: A Painter's Approach to Quilt Design • Velda Newman with Christine Barnes